Dear Mr. Landes

*Hope, Hurt, and Honest Letters
that Changed a Teacher's Life*

ROD LANDES

Performance Publishing Group
McKinney, TX

Copyright © 2025
Rod Landes

All Worldwide Rights Reserved.

All rights reserved. No part of this publication may be reproduced, stored in a retrieval system or transmitted, in any form or by any means, electronic, mechanical, recorded, photocopied, or otherwise, without the prior written permission of the copyright owner, except by a reviewer who may quote brief passages in a review.

ISBN:
978-1-967451-49-4 (paperback)

DEDICATION

To my beloved parents, Dr. Dean and
Patricia Landes Halmuth, both dearly missed.
And to my sister, Danita Illene Landes Bussey.

CONTENTS

Dedication   iii
Acknowledgments   vii
Letter From the Author   ix

PART I: THE MAKING OF A LIFE TEACHER

Chapter 1	From Lost Teen to English Teacher	1
Chapter 2	Discovering Purpose Through Speech and Affirmation	5
Chapter 3	Elliott and the Shift to Life Teaching	9

PART II: WHAT I'VE LEARNED ABOUT TEENAGERS

Chapter 4	What Teens Secretly Need	17
Chapter 5	What They Wish Adults Knew	28
Chapter 6	How to Help Them Grow	32

PART III: DEAR MR. LANDES LETTERS

Chapter 7	Anxiety	41
Chapter 8	Death	44
Chapter 9	Little Things That Are Big Things	48
Chapter 10	Family Relationships	52
Chapter 11	Fathers	59
Chapter 12	Friendship	70
Chapter 13	Young Love and First Relationships	72
Chapter 14	Sex and Teen Pregnancy	82
Chapter 15	Coming Out	86
Chapter 16	Depression	89
Chapter 17	A Special Case	96

Chapter 18 Goals and Aspirations	101
Chapter 19 Taking Responsibility	104
Chapter 20 Fears	107
Chapter 21 Pain	111
Chapter 22 Heroes	117
Chapter 23 Prayers	124
A Checklist for Dealing With Teens	129
I Believe	133
About the Author	135

ACKNOWLEDGMENTS

I want to thank my wife, Debbie, who has made me a better teacher, a better man, and a better everything.

My sons, Wyatt and Preston, who have grown into fine young men.

My former students. I taught more than 6,000 students during my career, many of whom wrote me letters and inspired these ideas.

LETTER FROM THE AUTHOR

I have been a high school teacher for over twenty-seven years, teaching English and Speech and coaching teens in Debate. I have taught at nine different schools in California's Central Valley and have taught over 6,000 students.

I am a father of two sons, Wyatt and Preston, now thirty-five and twenty-nine years old.

I have been around teenagers for a long time. I hear people saying, "What can be done about our teenagers?" They are thought to be generally lazy, bored, and apathetic.

I can relate to them because I've spent most of my adult life teaching, listening to, and raising them. Most importantly, I was once one of them.

I hated school. I hated English. I was a very average student, earning Bs, Cs, and Ds. My favorite classes were History and any class where my teacher was friendly and showed their humanity.

I thought I was ugly, stupid, and would never be successful at anything. I knew I was a failure. I had very low self-esteem, zero self-confidence, and no motivation. I was borderline suicidal, depressed, and had absolutely no positive vision for my life. I had very few friends and didn't know where I would end up. I felt like a loser. It was the teachers who cared as much about me as they did about the subjects they taught that pulled me through.

With the help of those teachers and a bit of stubborn willpower, I managed to graduate and eventually earned my degree to become a teacher myself.

For the past twelve years, I have stood outside my door at my current school, shaking the hands of my students as they enter my classroom.

At the beginning of each year, I acknowledge that many of them walk around all day and think, "No one even knows I exist." I tell them I know they exist, and I'm glad they are in my classroom.

As I shake their hands, I can usually tell the kind of day they are having—if they're sad, whether they've been crying, if they are angry, or whatever their emotional state at the moment. I often tell them, "If you don't want to tell me, write down what's going on so I can see if I can help you."

I have compiled a collection of student-written letters. All names and schools have been removed so that the letter writer may remain anonymous. But these are real students with real emotions. Real hurts and real problems. Some had no hope, were hurting, and felt helpless about their present and their future. It is a miracle some of them are still walking among us today. I want you, my readers, to see our youth. Their struggles. Their concerns.

I affectionately call this collection. Dear Mr. Landes.

PART I

The Making of a Life Teacher

CHAPTER

1

From Lost Teen to English Teacher

Somehow, I graduated from high school.

I was out of high school for six years before I decided to go to college. I started at Modesto Junior College by taking a math class during summer school, and I received a 101% in the class! Math was never my strength, so that gave me a huge boost of confidence, and I enrolled full-time in the fall of 1986.

I wasn't sure what I wanted to do, but I had always loved history, so I thought maybe I'd enjoy being a history teacher.

My dad was a doctor, my grandfather was a doctor, and my mom was a nurse, so I considered medicine, but I soon found out that I didn't enjoy Math or the Sciences, and I quickly gave up that idea.

I also considered becoming a counselor. I took a Psychology class, and I enjoyed the class, but I wasn't sure I wanted to listen to people's problems all day long. During a presentation, the instructor said, "You would be a great teacher!" The seed to teach was planted from the comments of one teacher.

I took a history class, and the instructor was not inspiring. I'd often almost fall asleep during his lectures. He knew his stuff, but he wasn't getting his stuff into me. I often thought I could teach it better than he was. I still wasn't sure what I wanted to do, but the idea of being a History teacher was rapidly fading!

I asked some friends who were also enrolled at MJC which English instructor I should take.

They all said, "Take Mr. Higgs; Mr. Jim Higgs."

So, I enrolled in Mr. Higgs' English 101 class. On the first day of class, he walked in wearing Birkenstock sandals, no socks, a Hawaiian shirt, and Levis with a hole in the knee. He had a beard, a mustache, glasses, shoulder-length hair, and was wearing a hat with a tassel dangling from the side. Not a guy I would automatically cuddle up to!

The first thing we did was put all our chairs in a circle. Instead of the traditional grammar and writing class, we had a discussion class, where we talked about a story or article we had read. It was the most excited and engaged I'd ever been in a class—especially an English class—and I was inspired.

I thought, "I think I could do this!" This is where I first decided to be a teacher!

I took another class with Mr. Higgs—English 102. I took English 103 with Mr. Phillips. I enjoyed learning to write, think, and articulate my thoughts and arguments in words, both spoken and on paper. My thoughts of becoming a history teacher began to erode and lean more toward English.

I graduated from MJC and transferred to California State University, Stanislaus, to further my studies in English. I studied writing, grammar, and syntax, and the rest of my classes were literature classes: British Authors Before and After 1800, American Literature, Children's Literature, Women's Literature, Critical Approaches to Literature, and Shakespeare. I rounded this off with journalism and drama classes. I was taking the Waiver program, which would allow me to teach Journalism, Speech, Drama, and English.

I graduated in the Spring of 1990 with a degree in English. This was all the training I needed to become an English teacher at that time. I never learned how to teach anyone to read or how to teach grammar lessons, but I would soon be a full-on English teacher!

I enrolled in the Student Teacher program at Stanislaus State, and the program was held at Manteca High School. The first-semester classes were spent in the classrooms, observing various teachers and tutoring individual students one-on-one. During my observations, I quickly determined that the best English teachers at Manteca High School were Virgil Dughi and Bonnie Lee.

The following semester, I took over Virgil's Sophomore Honors English class and Bonnie's Senior English class for my practicum. I have used the excellent advice these two teachers gave me in my classroom every day since.

Bonnie said, "Never start talking or teaching until everyone is ready to listen." To this day, I wait until it is totally quiet before I begin teaching.

Virgil said, "Rod, you are an easy-going guy, and when they are not working, you need to know how to get the class back again." I never have to yell, and I rarely raise my voice. I am thankful for these two pure gems of teaching wisdom.

After completing the Student Teacher program, I was now ready to start my teaching career. I submitted several applications all over the area, and then I came across an advertisement for a summer student exchange program. I called the number, met with the director, and was hired. My job was to teach and find host homes for twenty-five girls from Sasebo, Japan, for a month. It was my first taste of independent teaching. I taught the girls for half the day, then took them on field trips for the rest of the day. We explored the Hershey Chocolate Factory, Manteca Water Slide, Yosemite, and San Francisco. When it came time to take the girls back to San Francisco, I never cried so hard in my life, realizing I would never see these girls again, as they lived clear around the world.

I applied to several more places, but when the fall school year of 1991 was about to begin, I still didn't have a job. The day before school was to start, I got a call from Beyer High School about a long-term substitute position. A teacher, Sue Ionnedes, had cancer and was on leave. I started the year teaching sophomore and senior English. A week later, Mr. Tom Knight, another English teacher from Beyer, was hired to be an assistant principal at Modesto High. Mr. Flesuras, the principal at Beyer, came in to observe my teaching and later called me to his office. He said, "We're not sure how long Sue will be out, but we know Tom will be out all year, so we want you to take over his classes!" So, the next week, I started teaching all the junior English classes.

My teaching career had begun. I taught at Beyer that year, and the next fall, a brand-new, sixty-six-million-dollar high school opened. I applied for the 60% English/40% Speech position and was accepted. Johansen High School was equipped with all the bells and whistles, including a teacher computer and four student computers in every classroom. I taught at Johansen from 1992 until 2005.

CHAPTER

2

Discovering Purpose Through Speech and Affirmation

I enjoyed my years at Johnasen High, and discovered that I had a talent for coaching Speech. In the summer of 1998, I had two students qualify for the National Speech tournament in St. Louis: Morgan Grunerud and Peter Stone. Both came home National Champions—Peter in Impromptu and Morgan in Expository.

Their success prompted me to want to do even better, and I realized that if I wanted to be a great speech coach, I ought to learn about great coaches. So, all summer, I read biographies and autobiographies of great sports coaches—Woody Hayes, Don Shula, Tom Landry, Joe Paterno, John Wooden, Phil Jackson, Dean Smith, Sparky Anderson, Earl Weaver, Paul Bear Bryant, Vince Lombardi, and Jerry Tarkanian. All these coaches had won championships and had achieved the pinnacle of success, and all of them, I discovered, had certain things in common.

They all embodied determination, courage, perseverance, stamina, fear, and dedication, and they all set goals and practiced using affirmations. The concept of using affirmations appealed to me, and I began practicing them in my daily life. One of my favorites is:

> "If a man is called to be a street sweeper, he should sweep streets even as Michelangelo painted, or Beethoven played music, or Shakespeare wrote poetry. He should

sweep streets so well that all the hosts of heaven and earth will pause to say, here lived a great street sweeper who did his job well."

~ *Martin Luther King Jr.*

The practice produced noticeably positive results in my life, and I knew it was something that could help my students, as well.

I first started teaching the use of affirmations in the fall of 2001 with my Speech students, but quickly started introducing the concept to all of my students. At the beginning of each year, and after Christmas break, I gave them this to consider:

I AM A PROMISE

I am a promise, I am a possibility,
I am a great big bundle of potentiality.
I am talented,
I am attractive,
I am focused,
I am positive,
I am fearless,
I am smart,
I make good choices,
I am respectful,
I am responsible,
I am successful,
I am the standard by which excellence is measured,
And because I am,
I have a bright future,
Because I am a promise, I am a possibility.
I am a great big bundle of potentiality!

I met some initial resistance, but the students complied, and I did a new affirmation every week. Over the years, many of my students told me how meaningful those affirmations were in their lives and how they kept them, even years later. One affirmation I often offered my students was:

> "To one degree or another, most people are afraid of making big changes in their lives, even if those changes mean gaining something better... Any kind of change involves risk... Fear of risk often blocks any possibility of real success and fulfillment."
>
> ~ Denis Waitley

I ran into a former student at Target one day, who asked if I was still doing affirmations. I told him I was, and he quoted, "All change involves risk."

Later that year, I was in charge of watching graduation speeches. Seven of the ten students in my classes were giving speeches, and they all spoke about using affirmations. The mold had been set, and I have been practicing affirmations in my class, every day, every period, for the past sixteen years.

The next year, I attended a *Get Motivated* Seminar at the Cow Palace in San Francisco. Rudy Giuliani, Ronnie Lott, Joe Montana, Zig Ziglar, Jerry Lewis, Jessica Lynch, and Krish Dharma all spoke at this event.

Krish Dharma told us how he had been in the audience one time and aspired to be on stage one day. Zig Ziglar told us about Automobile University[1], a concept of using the time one spends commuting to work or traveling to listen to educational or motivational material. I had acquired several tape series from my Grandpa Boone, but had yet to listen to them. After the seminar, I listened to them and others and began applying the concepts to my life.

Pete Herrmann, the father of one of my Speech students, asked me if I had ever read *Think and Grow Rich*[2]. I hadn't, so I bought it and quickly consumed the information. It changed my life and my way of thinking.

In January 2005, I was at a State Speech council meeting in San Diego, and I saw a book at the airport called <u>The Success Principle: How to Get From Where You Are to Where You Want to Be,</u> by Jack Canfield[3], co-creator of *Chicken Soup for the Soul*. This book radically changed

---

[1] *Automobile University by Zig Ziglar,* getmotivation.com, 2025
[2] Hill, N. (2005). *Think and Grow Rich,* Tarcher Publishing.
[3] Canfield, J. (2015). *The Success Principles: How to Get from Where You Are to Where You Want to Be*, Mariner Books.

my life. Ideas such as "believe in yourself," "keep your eye on the prize," "ask, ask, ask," and "reject rejection" resonated with me. These were all concepts I had been lacking, which had held me back for my whole life. These kinds of motivational speakers had completely changed my perspective on life over the past few years, and I began to believe that my purpose was to pass that hope and inspiration on to others.

In February, I met a couple at a *Weekend to Remember* seminar in Stockton, and the idea of going into business took hold of me.

In June of 2005, I left my teaching position at Johansen and started a motivational speaking company. I hired a speech coach, and he advised me to set a goal of how many people I wanted to speak to that year. 1,000? 10,000? I set a goal to speak to 50,000 people over the next year and a half. In that time, I ended up speaking to over 200 groups and 9,000 people. I loved it, but I wasn't making enough money.

Over this time, I saw dozens of my former students, and they would always tell me how I had been their favorite teacher. I often heard, "I don't remember very many teachers, but I remember you." As much as I loved speaking and inspiring people, I missed teaching, and the seeds of returning to the classroom were planted once again. Perhaps that's where my real purpose lies—to offer young people hope, inspiration, and the tools to grow.

CHAPTER

3

Elliott and the Shift to Life Teaching

In February 2007, a long-term sub opportunity became available at Elliott Alternative Education, and I started teaching again.

Elliott Alternative Education School has long been known as the school for the bad kids—the problem kids, the kids nobody knows what to do with—and as a last-chance school. It was a tough school, with fights every day and rampant drug use... and lots and lots of hurting kids.

Over the years, I'd sent many kids to Elliott—not bad kids, but usually just kids who were way behind on credits. They might have fallen behind because of an illness, a death in the family, a learning disability, a lack of motivation, attendance issues, or many, many reasons that I had failed to see in my previous years of teaching.

I knew kids had issues, but I'd never encountered so many troubled kids in my past teaching positions. I remember talking to many of my kids and hearing their stories. One of their parents had medical issues, so the child became the primary caregiver. One of their parents had died, and they had to work. Others would let me know that they were home alone because both of their parents worked. It went on and on — so many troubled kids.

I discovered that I loved working with the low-level kids—the English language learners, Resource students, and basic-level kids.

While I have never taught a GATE class or an Advanced Placement class, I have taught a Speech class and coached a speech team for many years. Those classes are usually filled with the overachievers, the kids I affectionately call the "Movers and Shakers"—Student Body officers, band and orchestra students, athletes, and the "brainiacs."

For fourteen years, I taught English and Speech. I had 2,800 kids go through my classroom. I loved them all. I laughed with them, cried with them, visited them if they were in the hospital, went to funerals of parents, was invited to graduation parties, and eventually, weddings. I attended their games, their dances, and now, I've even been to some of their funerals.

But for fourteen years, I never really knew how much many of them were hurting; how many of them struggled to even get to school! How some of them had their addictions, how depressed they were, how discouraged they were, how defeated they felt.

The reason I failed to see this was because I was one of them. I was defeated. I was depressed. I had no successful vision of my future. I didn't see them because I was hurting. I did not feel heard. I was—or at least I thought I was—voiceless and basically non-existent. I was hurting, helpless, and hopeless.

Over the course of those fourteen years, I had sought help from counselors and advisers, and I began to work on myself and deal with my rejection and abandonment issues. That, along with the coaching/motivational learning I did, started to turn my life around and helped me see others more clearly as well. As I began to focus less on myself, I started to see other hurting, voiceless, non-existent people, too!

By the time I began teaching at Elliott, I saw my students as more than 'bad,' 'tough,' or unmotivated kids. I saw their pain and how helpless, hopeless, and hurting they were. Between the start of my placement in February 2007 and the end of the school year in the first week of June, I had quite an education. In those five months, the heart of my teaching took a turn for the better.

I remember giving a standardized test in March—a test that should have taken three hours. Most kids were done in fifteen minutes. Many kids just bubbled in the bubbles, either because they couldn't read, couldn't comprehend, or didn't care. They were looking down the barrel of a gun, ready to be blown away, and they were totally and utterly defenseless.

Yes, Elliott has its daily fights, and its population included gang bangers, druggies, skaters, and the like, but there were also kids who were scared at that school, trying to stay unnoticed and undetected, so they wouldn't be called out, threatened, or bullied.

I'm not sure how it started, or why, or what the inspiration was, but it was at Elliott where I started shaking kids' hands as they entered my classroom. I would stand at my door and shake the students' hands as they came into my classroom and as they left each day. I was teaching in a portable classroom, and there was another building close by, across the way. I was quite amazed and astonished when a student from another classroom would come over to my class, shake my hand, and then go to their classroom. I think some students were tardy to their other class because they wanted and needed a handshake from me.

Now, I always tell my kids on the first day of class that one of the reasons I shake their hands each day is because I know that a number of them walk around our school campus feeling like nobody even knows they exist! They feel unseen, unheard, unnoticed!

I tell them that I know that they are there, and I'm glad they are in my classroom. If I'm busy at my computer or my desk before class and not standing at the door, I always have students who come over for a handshake. If they come in after the bell rings, they always get a handshake when they come through the door.

Touch is one of the five love languages, as described by Gary Chapman[4]. Shaking their hands is a way I can show I care about them. I've had a few students who were uncomfortable shaking hands, so we'd do a fist bump instead. I want them to *know* that I'm aware they're in my classroom and that it matters. I always take the time to go around the room to show them the proper handshake technique, and most of my students know how to give a proper, good, firm handshake.

A good firm handshake, with good eye contact and an erect posture, shows that you have confidence and are proud of yourself.

A wimpy, dead-fish handshake says, "I am insecure. I am a victim.

---

[4] Chapman, G. (2010). *The 5 Love Languages: The Secret to Love That Lasts*, Northfield Publishing

I hate myself. I have very low self-confidence." Truth be told, when you offer me that kind of handshake, I want to smack you!

Our first impressions are huge, and one way we can make a good first impression is with a firm, solid handshake.

I'm not sure who I hugged first or when, but when a person comes to me with tears in their eyes, what am I to do? I give out lots and lots of hugs.

I realize I do that at some risk, with abuse and harassment in the news way too often about educators who took advantage of their trusted positions in our schools and communities. I have been cautioned by various school administrators, and I take their counsel very seriously. Yet, what can I do when a child is hurting and crying right in front of me?

I recall having a junior girl in my class who brought in a little freshman girl to talk to me. The girl was having family problems, so I listened to her, gave her my advice, and gave her a hug. Her locker was just a few yards from my door, so I would hug her every time I saw her. Sometimes, I hugged her five times in a day! I asked her one time, "Do you ever get tired of me giving you hugs?" I'll never forget her response. "You're the only person who hugs me!" Wow! No wonder some of our students feel so unloved, so ugly, so worthless!

One of the freshmen girls on my Speech team gave me a handshake plaque, thanking me as a teacher, and one of the things mentioned on that board was that she was thankful for my hugs.

Over the years, I've hugged hundreds of kids—possibly thousands—boys and girls alike. Some kids get physically punished, hit, mistreated, and abused by their parents, so they might shy away from a hug. Some may have been physically or sexually abused, so I try to be sensitive to personal space and other issues that they may be fighting and dealing with.

I remember one girl who only wanted a fist bump at the beginning of the school year. About December, she approached my desk to thank me for my kindness and for helping her. I started to tear up, and I asked if I could give her a hug. She had been cutting herself and was depressed and suicidal. I am happy to say, whenever I see this girl, she always gives me the biggest hugs.

Another one of my former freshmen girls, now a sophomore and no longer enrolled in my class, runs and almost knocks me over as she gives me a hug whenever she sees me.

In our technological world of computers, phones, and iPods, we are losing the positive, physical, one-on-one contact that used to be a part of our society. I do everything I can to keep real communication alive and thriving in my classroom.

At Elliott, I saw many kids who had no hope for their futures. I remember asking one of my girls what she wanted to be when she got older. I forget what she said she wanted to be, but I recall her saying she couldn't because of something that had happened in her past. She was sixteen! At sixteen, she had already given up on her dreams and her future. She was a victim of her past. I know adults who are still victims of their pasts. I have an eighty-five-year-old relative who told me, "I was never very smart." Even at eighty-five years old, he still believed he had little to offer the world because he didn't think he was smart enough!

I remember being exposed to Howard Gardner's seven intelligences [5] and learning about how we all have different intelligences, and we all learn differently. We teach one way in our educational institutions, yet we have people who learn best in a variety of ways. Many students in my classes have trouble taking tests, sometimes because they have a learning disability. I remember taking a math class in high school, and it all making perfect sense. I was eating it up! Then, I'd get home, open the book to a lesson I had just been taught, and it looked like a foreign language. I'd wonder, what in the world is this stuff? I feel your pain, friends, I've been there, done that, and I understand.

My students at Elliott weren't just students I was teaching English to. These were children who had lost hope, needed or wanted help, and who were hurting. These students, and my experiences in this school, changed my approach and philosophy toward teaching. I am no longer simply an English teacher. I am a Life teacher!

I teach life lessons through literature in my English classes, and I am a minister to those who are helpless, hopeless, and hurting. For way too long, I never knew I had classrooms full of them. They are not only in our schools, but in our churches and our homes. Everywhere I look, I see people who are helpless, hopeless, and hurting, and as a teacher, I intend to offer help, hope, and comfort to those who are hurting.

---

[5] Gardner, H. (1983). *Frames of the Mind: The Theory of Multiple Intelligences*, New York: Basic Books

PART II

What I've Learned About Teenagers

CHAPTER

4

What Teens Secretly Need

Teenagers need to be noticed.

People love to be noticed, and they want to feel special. If a student misses a day, I tell them, the next time I see them, "I missed you." I try to notice new haircuts, new shoes, the outfits they are wearing, or that their team won. Kids love to be noticed, and they love compliments. It's easy to find fault and focus on all their mistakes, but it's important to look for the good and acknowledge that. When a student has a birthday, I play them a birthday song, and give them a chocolate hug and a kiss. Catch them being good, and be liberal and sincere with your compliments.

I always greet my kids at the door to welcome them to my classroom, but also to observe what kind of day they are having. If they appear sad or angry, or if they have been crying, I know early on and can keep an eye on them during class. I let them know I see them and ask how I can help. If they don't want to tell me, I encourage them to write me a letter, so I know how best to help them. Often, they do.

Most teenagers—and maybe most people in this world—feel unnoticed, and those who most need attention will often go to drastic measures to get it.

We see it splashed all over the TV, newspapers, and social media—people making desperate attempts to be noticed. Why do they do stupid and foolish things? They want to be noticed and remembered for something.

In all my years of teaching, I haven't lost a student from my classroom. Maybe it's because I pay attention and notice them.

They need to be loved and respected.

I may be unique, but I believe that to gain respect, you have to show respect. If you want love, you need to be the first to show it.

I have received great love and mercy in my life, so perhaps I have more to give, but I love my students even before I meet them. I consider them my sons and daughters. I care for and love my own sons very much, so shouldn't my students receive the same treatment?

I believe everyone deserves respect, even though they may do things that are disrespectful. I never yell at my students, and I never talk down to, ridicule, or demean them.

If I have an issue with a student's classroom behavior, I ask them to stop. If they don't, I ask again. If it continues, I ask them to go into the hall. I wait a few minutes, then I go to them and ask, "Have I done something you don't like?" Usually, it's, "Oh, no, Mr. Landes." I then explain to them what I'm not liking and why I sent them into the hall. I never make fun of them or treat them any differently once they are back in my classroom.

I rarely give out referrals. I could, but I choose to use respect and unconditional love instead.

They will test that love and respect.

Teenagers need to be noticed, loved, and respected, and yet they will test it. Do you really love me unconditionally? Do you really care?

I can't tell you how many students tell me that their parents are self-absorbed, work two jobs, or are addicts. Some have so many distractions in their lives that they don't have time for their kids.

To parents: When was the last time you went to an event your child was involved in? When did you sit down just to listen? When was the last time you met your child's friends? Had them over to the house? When was the last time you complimented them rather than noticing what they did wrong?

I've heard kids say, "The only time my parent notices me is when I get in trouble, when I get bad grades, or when I haven't met their mark or expectation."

Teenagers are very self-absorbed, constantly thinking of what they want right now. During this time of immaturity, they need our patience, mercy, grace, tolerance, and lots of unconditional love.

Words we say in the heat of the moment and actions we take can have lasting repercussions. Remember who the adult is and act accordingly. If we want respect, we have to be the first to show it.

Even though they resist affection, they secretly yearn for it.

When was the last time you hugged your child? When did you show any kind of positive affection?

I give lots of handshakes and hugs. Most of my students love them.

I often sit in my classroom early before school starts, and I can't tell you how many kids have come into my classroom crying, just needing a safe place to land, or asking for a hug.

It says you are important to me. You are valuable. You are noticed.

Life is tough for all of us, and for teens, it is especially tough because they don't always have the maturity or the tools to deal with the pressures they often face. What would our world be like if it were softer and gentler, more caring, more considerate? In our world full of hate, intolerance, and violence, we are getting further and further away from face-to-face, real, genuine, and honest relationships.

I give hugs to lots of people—boys and girls, the homeless lady in the McDonald's parking lot, the grieving mother at Walmart, the single gal at church, crying after a sermon. All of them thanked me for my hug and had tears in their eyes as they said it. Give heartfelt and sincere affection.

They want to be treated as though they have value.

Teenagers are just pre-adults who want to be treated the way we adults like to be treated.

How many times have you said, "I've told you a hundred times to… (fill in the blank)"? After being a communication teacher for twenty years, I've learned that the listener is rarely at fault — rather, it's the one speaking! The message is obviously not getting through to your audience. Instead of repeating yourself a hundred times, ask them if they understand and have them repeat back what they heard.

Some of us talk to our kids as if they are a nuisance, in our way, and a bother to us. Who likes to be spoken to like a little child? Who likes to be talked to as if we were an idiot? NOBODY

Talk to them like you would like to be talked to! Our tone of voice says volumes. Do we use sarcasm? Do we cuss and use abusive, obscene language? Do we yell over someone else? Our voice level has a lot to do with what is understood, remembered, and retained.

Check our voices, our tone, our words. They have much more power than we realize! Use these tools for good!

Are we approachable? Can they tell us anything and everything without feeling embarrassed or fear of being ridiculed?

How do you like to be treated? How do you like to be talked to? How teenagers are treated as they grow up largely shapes how they assume the rest of the world lives and how they'll treat others.

Treat them with grace, kindness, love, mercy, and respect. If you want that kind of treatment, be the first to show it!

We treat them with value because they are ours, and they are the future of our world. What kind of world do you want to grow old in? Kids who feel valued will grow into adults who see the value in others.

They want to be told they are beautiful and smart.

One of my favorite Bible verses is: "As a man thinks in his heart, so is he." (Proverbs 23:7). How we think about ourselves has a huge impact on who we will become in life.

It's been my observation that most students have very low self-esteem, even those students who are naturally beautiful and talented. They hear it more than most, yet there is a part of them that doesn't believe the compliments they receive.

We should be sincere and effusive with our praise and compliments.

Some might argue that the person will become proud or egotistical. I get lots of compliments, maybe more than most, and yet the lonely little boy inside still wonders if the person really means it, or if they feel sorry for me.

I have yearbooks full of kind words from my students, and it's very hard for me to believe what my students think of me, even though I know I've made a huge impact on many lives!

Giving abundant compliments will not make your child an egotistical monster. It will help them focus on their strengths, take pride in their efforts, and find the confidence to take risks and build skills.

Look for ways to encourage someone to do better! Negative comments tend to really unsettle me, but I can coast a long time on a good compliment!

I remember eating at Taco Bell one day, and the cashier had a great smile! I'm a sucker for a great smile, so I told her I liked her smile. As I ate, I watched the lady I had just complimented. She beamed! She wore a bigger smile than the one I had just complimented her on.

Dale Carnegie's first principle in his book *How to Win Friends & Influence People*[6] is: Don't criticize, condemn, or complain. If we follow this, we have more time to compliment, encourage, and work on solving problems.

I'm an encourager. That's what I do. Notice the good in people rather than focusing on the bad or the things you disapprove of. Tell them the good things you see in them. This small act of kindness could change a life.

They want to know that when they fail, you still love them unconditionally.

Teenagers make all kinds of stupid mistakes. They fail tests or classes, they get speeding tickets, they get into accidents, they get drunk,

---

[6] Carnegie, D. *How to Win Friends & Influence People.* (1990) Pocket Books

they get arrested and thrown into jail, they get pregnant, they have abortions. The list is endless. They fail, sometimes dramatically and with disastrous consequences!

When they fail, often their first thought is: My parents are going to kill me. Their fear is real because they don't know the limits of your love. Our kids need to know they are loved, especially right after they have failed big time.

It's at the worst time in our lives, when we are faced with disappointments of our children, that our love is challenged. Do they know you love them unconditionally? Even when they screw up and fail miserably? Or is your love conditional? I'll love you if… I'll love you when… If you didn't do this activity or get these grades, then I'd love you.

Our kids need to know they are loved, always, and even though. Our pride is often threatened when our kids disappoint us or do stupid things. Remember, it's not about you, your reputation, or social standing. It's about them.

They need to be told you love them, again and again.

We hear it tossed about all the time: "I love you!" But are our actions consistent with our words? Do we say loving words with a loving tone? Do we see the good in our children? Is our life one of service and giving, or is it one of taking and complaining?

When our children are upset, mad, resentful, or angry, we need to ask ourselves: when was the last time we told them we loved them?

They need to hear it over and over again!

I don't remember hearing 'I love you' very much in my life. I often wondered: Am I loved? Why don't I feel loved? Why am I always alone?

Life is tough, and teens need to know that home is a "safe place to land." Too many kids live in a war zone, with words flying like bullets, and everyone wondering if they are valued, treasured, or loved.

If you haven't done it lately, tell your children you love them, and tell them soon and often. Then, tell them again. There should never be a question in a child's mind whether they are loved by their parents or not.

DEAR MR. LANDES

They like it when you tell them you are praying for them.

So many hurting students in my classroom have written letters to me about their struggles. Sometimes, I don't know what to say or do, but often in these moments, I tell them I will keep them in my prayers.

I usually have my students write a one-page life story in the first week of school, because I believe that if I know where they are, I can better teach them.

I've read about parents who have died, parents going through a divorce, learning disabilities, if they have just moved to the area, if they haven't seen a parent for a long time, if they are adopted, or a foster child. I know who to keep my eyes on and who needs extra attention.

I am also a firm believer that if a child has a traumatic, drastic issue going on in their lives, they are going to be less interested in whatever I have to offer in class that day.

I heard a quote early in my teaching career:

> People won't care how much you know until they know how much you care.
>
> ~ *Theodore Roosevelt*

Many people will die today, wondering if their lives made a difference. I'm happy to say, I've had testimony from many people about how a kind word, a thoughtful action, a hug, a prayer, or a note of encouragement helped them in their time of need. I know I've made a difference in my world by being caring, merciful, and kind to people who need to know there are still people in this world who care.

Pray for your students, and let them know you are praying for them, even if they pretend it's weird. I've had students come to me and ask me to pray for them. Whatever you can do to bring them comfort and to let them know they are loved... do it.

The hardest lessons are learned from mistakes.

Nobody likes losers, and everybody loves winners. Yet, as I've read biographies and autobiographies of successful people, I've discovered that they all suffered major failures in their lives.

Henry Ford, Walt Disney, Milton Hershey, H.J. Heinz, and P.T. Barnum—all massive business successes who went bankrupt early on in their lives.

Thomas Edison failed a thousand times in trying to develop the light bulb. People would ask him if he ever got discouraged, and he would say, "I have not failed. I've just found 10,000 ways that won't work!"[7]

Darren Hardy, the editor of Success Magazine, said one of the tools he used to become successful was to Embrace Failure. Early in his real estate career, he would try to get fifty no's a day. Amidst all the no's, there would be an eventual success.[8]

Abraham Lincoln was defeated eight times in his political career before he finally became the sixteenth President of the United States.

We don't fear failure as much as we fear rejection. We fear looking foolish or like a loser. But our kids need to know that the only failure is the person who gives up and doesn't give their all.

One of my favorite sayings is: If you really want to do something, you'll find a way. If you don't, you'll find an excuse.[9] As I reflect back on my life, I realize now how many excuses I made. "I don't have time." "I don't have money." "I'm tired." "I don't feel good." "I don't know how." "It's too hard." When our kids are faced with challenges or big projects, we need to teach them how to eat an elephant. One piece at a time! Just get started!

Since hearing this quote, I now always ask myself, "How badly do I want it? And what price am I willing to pay to get it?" We need to model this for our children and teach them to stop making excuses and start

---

[7] *Importance of Thomas Edison's Quotes*, thomasedison.org, 2024
[8] Hardy, D. *The Compound Effect: Jumpstart Your Income, Your Life, Your Success.* (2010) Success Media Books
[9] Jim Rohn – motivational speaker and self-help author. YouTube: *Five Habits That Changed My Life in 1 Week.* www.youtube.com/@JimRohnAcademy747

finding a way to make things happen. They need to know that taking risks and putting themselves out there is not a bad thing, and what looks like failure is actually simply learning. Allowing ourselves to 'fail' means having the confidence to try. Our kids need to know that they are safe and supported if they're ever going to take those chances.

We often underestimate our abilities. Norman Vincent Peale advises us to: Throw your heart over the bar, and your body will follow.[10] For too long, I had a weak mind and a failure mentality. I expected to fail, and I was afraid of success. I didn't understand that most people carry these huge self-doubts when they are young and immature.

When I was younger, I read a lot of books about famous people. At the time, I didn't realize how their early lives related to mine. Now, when I have my students read books about successful people, I have them focus on the years from birth to eighteen. All famous and successful people—their idols and superstars—sat in classrooms similar to theirs and survived failures and embarrassments similar to theirs. If they could do it, so can my students. My students often thank me for this valuable gold nugget!

They are secretly scared about their futures.

A high percentage of kids are scared about their futures. For freshmen, it's: Will I graduate? Sophomores stress about whether they'll pass their driver's license test. Juniors wonder if they'll be able to get a job. Seniors struggle with getting accepted into the college of their choice.

Where will I live? Will I get married? How will I pay my bills? On and on and on!

The solution to this problem is teaching them to have a positive vision of their future and to set short- and long-term goals.

I always encourage my students to visualize being seventy years old and sitting on their front porch, rocking their grandchild. I ask them to think: What have I done with my life? Where have I traveled? Who have I met? What accomplishments have I made in my lifetime?

---

[10] Peale, N.V. *The Power of Positive Thinking.* (2003) Touchstone Books

If they can get that picture firmly in their mind, they are well on their way to a successful future!

So many people don't know who they are, what they want, or how to get there. Success leaves tracks. Learn about other people you consider successful, and start doing what they have done. Ask questions, read books, and learn, learn, learn!

They want to know how to be successful.

I think everyone, when they come to the end of their lives, wants to know that their lives mattered—that their lives have been worthwhile.

We need to give kids the tools to accomplish that goal.

What does it take to be a success? That all depends on our definition of success. Whether it's to be happy, married, healthy, financially independent, capable, or self-reliant, all of these have different ways to be achieved.

They need to know your successes, but they also need to know about your struggles! They need to know what you did right and what you will never do again.

They need to know what you wished you had learned or done in high school, but didn't because you were too scared or couldn't.

They need to know your hardest moments, when you just about gave up, but willed yourself on to fight another day.

Life is tough, and if you live a life of ease now, they need to know what life was like before you made it to the top; what struggles you faced, what obstacles you overcame, how you survived. They need to know, they want to know, and they deserve to know!

I wish we, as educators, would place greater emphasis on teaching financial literacy, relationship-building skills, conflict management, stress reduction, time management, building resilience and toughness, and coping with unexpected circumstances. That is the education our children really need.

Charlie "Tremendous" Jones once said, "You'll be the same person five years from now as you are today except for two things: the people you meet and the books you read."[11] We need to teach our kids to be careful of the people they associate with and promote literacy at all costs. Their success as adults depends on it.

"Learn to earn, be teachable, be willing to fail, thrive."[12]

---

[11] *Five Years From Now....* Tracy Jones. Tremendousleadership.com. 2018
[12] Edmondson, A. *Right Kind of Wrong: The Science of Failing Well.* (2023) Simon Element/Simon Acumen

CHAPTER 5

What They Wish Adults Knew

They really want their parents to listen,
even though they are dead wrong.

Most people don't listen very well. We often listen just enough to quickly reply or rebut what is being said.

What would happen if we listened without casting judgment or giving a quick fix solution to whatever is being discussed?

Our teenagers are living in troubling times, and they need a listening ear, an understanding heart, and a shoulder to lean on. With social media so rampant, there are many voices out there, and if they can't talk to you, they will talk to somebody else.

Try to listen—turn off distractions, give them your full attention, make eye contact, and don't interrupt—to really hear their case and argument. They are trying to get along in this confusing world, and I see so many students who want and need to talk, but their parents are unapproachable.

Remember your life as a teenager and multiply it. They are living in a hurry-scurry world, and they need to vent about their lives, their fears, their concerns, their teachers, and maybe even you! Don't be defensive, and try to listen objectively.

They want to know what a true friend is.

In our world today, our minds and eyes are bombarded with information. The fabric of our society has been disintegrating for quite a while.

Leaders—politicians, teachers, preachers, neighbors, business owners, friends—who were once esteemed and trusted have broken our trust. We don't know who or what to trust. Kids want to know who is there for them, who they can rely on, and who has their backs.

Are you dependable? When you say you'll do something, do you do it? If you say you will be somewhere at a certain time, are you there? Do you gossip? Are you a blowhard full of hot air? Or are you a person of substance, a person who is honest and truthful? Are you modeling how to be a good friend?

I have lots of acquaintances, but very few real, close friends. Real friends hear with their hearts. They ask the tough questions and give wise advice that is helpful rather than hurtful. A true friend is someone who helps you, who encourages you to do the right thing, who listens, and isn't afraid to upset you if you are going off the rails.

> Be the kind of friend you want to have. "A friend is a stranger I have yet to meet!"
> ~ *William Butler Yeats*

To have friends, you must show yourself to be friendly! Smile, be happy!

They want to know what truth is, and they can tell if you don't know it.

Our teenagers are bombarded with information all day long, and they are asking the question: Who and what can I believe?

I was raised in a very strong, stable, loving Christian church community. I've never doubted the Bible or the existence of God, although I doubted my own abilities for far too long. I have a strong foundation of faith and belief. But many of our children aren't raised with that these days. With all the different voices out there, they want to know what is believable, what is truth, and what will endure.

A student once asked me, "Mr. Landes, how do we know which church or religion to belong to, and what to believe?" I said then, and I still say today, that a true seeker will always find truth!

If you want truth, seek it, pursue it, strive hard for it!

I am confident that who I am today is a product of my past. I might have been naturally kind, gentle, patient, loving, and merciful, but that was also the foundation I was taught and believed most of my life.

Seek the truth. It is there to be discovered by the truth seeker.

They notice the smallest things.

Kids notice a lot more than we realize. They are paying attention to our smallest moves, the words we say, and the actions we take. They notice!

One year, a group of my Speech students composed a book of what they affectionately called "Landesisms." I had forgotten I had even said them! I was embarrassed by some of the things I purportedly said!

They notice when our words don't match up with our actions. They notice what we do in our leisure time. They notice and know what our priorities really are. They notice when we are troubled or stressed, sad, or worried. They notice!

They notice how we drive, how we treat people, and how we react to difficulties and problems. They notice when we are caught in an untruth or if we are being hypocritical. They know if we are lying to them... and often to ourselves!

They notice what you wear, how you behave, and any little changes you make. And they expect you to notice those things in them! Two examples pop into my mind. One day, I was wearing a plaid shirt with lots of colors, and one of my boys said, "Pick a color, Mr. Landes." We all laughed. Another day, a girl came into my class, jumped in front of me, and asked, "Do you know what is different about me?" Really! A woman asking a man to notice anything different about her! REALLY!

They notice the littlest things, and that may be the reason they say, "You did it, so why can't I?" They notice many things we probably wish they wouldn't, but they notice.

After all these years of teaching, these are just a few of the things I've learned about teens. It is obviously not all-inclusive, but it's my tale on the teenagers I've loved and lived with on this incredible journey.

CHAPTER

6

How to Help Them Grow

They turn out to be pretty good adults.

I've been teaching for over twenty-six years, so my first students are now in their forties.

I've had the privilege of teaching many students who have gone on to college and are white-collar workers. They are doctors, teachers, lawyers, accountants, worldwide musicians and vocalists, business owners, and productive members of society.

I've taught many blue-collar workers as well—plumbers, electricians, carpenters, air-conditioning technicians, and auto mechanics. They work in stores and start their own businesses.

I have even taught a murderer... and I would never have thought it while teaching him. I loved him like a son, and I still do. I always hope he is okay.

I love going somewhere and seeing my students in the work arena. I went to the doctor, and a former student was the physician's assistant. I went to the Emergency Room, and a former student did my EKG. I found a former student working at the car wash. I've met them in restaurants, grocery stores, and gas stations.

I am on Facebook, and probably half of my Facebook friends are students or former students. I get emails periodically, with pictures of their travels, their weddings, their children, their homes, and their cars. I am so proud of my former students, and they are the first people I call if I have a need they can fulfill.

I always say, "I may not be your only teacher, but you will always be my student, and I'll be in your life as long as you need me."

Challenge them to be great.

So many people are happy to be average, and there is certainly nothing wrong with that. But what if someone convinced us we could be the best at whatever we chose to do?

I don't remember anyone ever telling me I could be great or I could be the best. I was raised in a community that prided itself on humility and the simple things in life. I was never pushed. Although I was surrounded by successful people—my dad and grandpa were both doctors, my mom was a nurse, my cousin was a physician's assistant, and another cousin was a preacher—I was largely alone in finding my way in life.

I was never taught how to handle money or build successful relationships. Much of what I've learned has been in the past fifteen years. And as an educator, I want to pass on what I've learned to future generations to help make their paths easier.

I am glad to talk about my failures, my weaknesses, my insecurities, and my very low self-esteem, as I know many of my students fight this very same battle! I'm also excited to share my successes, my ambitions, my strengths, my improved self-esteem, how I 'fixed' myself, and how I continue to reach for success. In sharing my journey, I push them to reach for the best they can become.

Find a young person and be a champion in their life. Spend time with them, ask them questions, tell them your stories. They need to know that success is possible, even if they are confused and failing now. They need to hear them.

Be a champion in their life.

How exactly can you be a champion to a teen? They need someone they can trust, someone they can call on, talk about their successes, and cry to about their defeats.

Looking back on my high school days, I was very alone. I wasn't a troublemaker, but I was very lonely. Mr. Myers, our school librarian, was someone who I knew cared about me. I spent lots of time in the library.

Most men don't have a good male friend or role model. Many don't have a good friend. A boy growing up without a male influence in the house suffers. It takes a man to teach a boy how to be a man. A woman, though she tries hard, cannot achieve that job.

A champion listens, asks the tough questions, and cares about the one he is in charge of.

My mentor, Vern Carson, a ninety-year-old man, married for over sixty years, invested hours into my life. I would spend one hour a week with Vern doing Bible Studies and reading books together, and his friendship helped me be a better man, husband, father, teacher, and leader. I knew I could cry, laugh, ask questions, and seek advice from this man, and he always had my best interest in mind. He was my champion.

Be a champion in a young person's life!

Give them more responsibility early.

In our urban world, kids often lack opportunities to engage in tasks and take responsibility. In rural farm communities, there are animals to care for, fields to plow, plant, and harvest, wood to cut, lawns to mow, and countless other jobs.

So, what can we do to teach our kids responsibility in urban settings, where many live with only small yards, if any? Will they learn it by texting, playing video games, or listening to music? I think not!

There are some easy ways to add responsibility and tasks. Have them learn to cook and prepare a meal, learn to wash clothes, feed and walk the dog, be on time, be honest, be real, and be true to their word. Teach them that if you say you will do it, do it!

So many people blame others for their failures or oversights, but one of the keys to successful living is taking responsibility. Don't blame your parents, teachers, preachers, friends, the government, road rage, or a hectic life. Take responsibility for your own words and actions. If they can't learn it as a youth, when will they ever learn it?

Teach them the value of a job well done.

I learned this lesson late in my life. I did things with a 'good enough' attitude. I never took pride in my work, believing it would never be good enough anyway. I didn't realize then that when people pushed me to do better, it wasn't criticism or failure; they were just trying to help me grow.

Somewhere in my early growing-up days, I lost any confidence I had in my ability to do things well, so I was always in a hurry to get tasks over with. I was a marginal student as a teenager, and I knew I wasn't smart academically at all. I tried to study and invested time, but it never gave me the reward I wanted or thought I needed.

I would get discouraged very easily, and any attempts to teach me were met with resistance because I was so insecure and had such low self-esteem. Usually, I was given a task and left alone to finish it. I hated being alone, and I couldn't wait to finish my task because I wanted to be around people. I see these same traits in my students all the time.

How can we get past our kids' insecurities and defensiveness and teach them the value of giving their all to a task?

Explain the expectations of the task, exactly! What is expected? Break the task down into easier steps, if necessary. Offer a reasonable timeline for completing the task. If you can show them and teach them what you expect, you have a better chance of getting the desired result.

And when they succeed, celebrate them! Show them you are proud of them. When their efforts are valued, they will want to try again... and harder.

They want to learn real-world life lessons.

I can't tell you how many students have told me, "You are the best teacher I've ever had!" I think it's because I am honest, transparent, open, and vulnerable.

Many people can't be because they are fearful that their past may come back to haunt them, maybe bringing guilt, embarrassment, and shame.

A person has to be wise with the information they share, of course, but I think it's important that our kids know about our failures as well as our successes. It's important that they know about our fears and how we manage them, and how we build our confidence.

They want to know —and I think they need to know —how to face the everyday challenges of life as an adult. They need role models and direct teaching in these crucial life lessons: Taxes, finances, credit, relationships, anger management, conflict resolution, applying for and keeping a job, buying and selling a house, car, etc., balancing a checkbook, and managing investments.

I was never taught any of these things in school or at home, and had to educate myself on these life lessons on my own, often the hard way. We can do better and make it easier for our kids.

They like to be told that they did a good job.

Our students face a unique challenge that was not a part of our reality when we were growing up. In the online world our kids navigate every day, everything is open to comment, and often negativity, criticism, and condemnation.

Even if a job is done well, somebody out there will, and often does, criticize what was done.

There is so much more negative energy than positive in our world that the bad often trumps the good. Even if we are complimented on a job well done, our negative mindset often overrules.

It has been said that it takes five positive comments to override one negative comment.[13] I get lots of encouragement, and yet one negative comment can get me all twisted around and in a funk!

I've learned how to get up and stay positive. There are people I know who will lift me up and give me encouragement. I read good books, listen to good music, hang around positive people, and I don't listen to the news very often.

---

[13] Benson, Kyle. *The Magic Relationship Ratio, According to Science*, Gottman.com, 2017

Be effusive with compliments, do it sincerely, and notice the good things that are done by those closest to you! Praise your kids when they've done a good job. They need all the encouragement they can get.

Let them laugh.

Life is tough, and our teenagers are bombarded with negative news, negative song lyrics, scary movies, and intense online pressure. They need to laugh.

They need to learn to laugh hardest at themselves. They need to learn to have a good sense of humor, but never to laugh at the expense of someone else's misfortune.

It's okay to do something to get them to laugh. Babies smile and laugh often, but as we get older and more mature, we laugh less and less.

Laughter is the joy and song of the soul, and a good laugh is often all that's needed to lift a 'down' mood, relieve stress, or give someone a fresh perspective. We all need a good laugh once in a while—the kind of laughter that gives us a stomachache and makes us want to throw up. And shared laughter has the bonus of making us feel a part of something positive. I must confess, I don't laugh a lot, but I also don't get angry very often. But when I do laugh, it always feels good, and our teens need this 'feel good' feeling.

> "Laugh, and the world laughs with you; weep, and you weep alone."
> *~ Ella Wheeler Silcox, from the poem Solitude*

They like to hear poetry.

In my classroom, I always give out an affirmation every week, and for the past few years, I've also included a motivational, inspirational poem.

The poem *Don't Quit*[14] saved me when I was at the lowest point of my life! Now, I give this poem to my students at the end of each year. It helped me, and I'm sure it's helped others along the way.

> When things go wrong, as they sometimes will,
> When the road you're trudging seems all uphill,
> When the funds are low and the debts are high,
> And you want to smile, but you have to sigh,
> When care is pressing you down a bit,
> Rest if you must, but don't you quit.
> Life is strange with its twists and turns,
> As every one of us sometimes learns,
> And many a failure comes about,
> When he might have won had he stuck it out.
> Don't give up, though the pace seems slow,
> You may succeed with another blow.
> Success is failure turned inside out –
> The silver tint of the cloud of doubt.
> And you never can tell just how close you are,
> It may be near when it seems so far.
> So stick to the fight when you're hardest hit –
> It's when things seem worst that you must not quit.

I have a collection of poems that I have used over the years, and many of my former students have told me they kept all the affirmations, poems, and quotes I gave them, and when they hit a tough spot in their life, they pull the collection out, refresh, and keep moving.

I have written poems over the years, and I have learned to love poetry. Sometimes, words that are bled all over the paper, from people who have been there, too, can help us feel less alone in the world.

Words have power. They have rhythm and rhyme, and in the heat of the day, a phrase, a verse, a song, or a poem can keep us moving forward.

---

[14] Guest, E.A. *Don't Quit*. (1921) Detroit Free Press

PART III

Dear Mr. Landes Letters

CHAPTER 7

Anxiety

Over the years, I have greeted my students at the door each morning, checking in with them to see how they're coming into my class and into their day. If they are sad, angry, or needing some sort of support, I often encourage them to write me a letter so I can help, if I can.

Our students/children, especially those in demographics like Elliott, are under tremendous strain, trying to grow up, often without sufficient support. They live with more stress than any generation that came before them. They show up with confusion, frustration, and fear, and they are often under a surprising degree of pressure – more than most typical adults could easily handle. The added constant scrutiny of the online world makes their lives even harder.

By sharing their letters, I hope to show how much our kids struggle and how badly they need us. The teen years are often the hardest in anyone's life, and having people on our side who love us unconditionally, are willing to listen, offer encouragement and support, and guide us toward maturity and adulthood can make all the difference.

Some of these letters are funny—typical teen love letters and angst. But many of them are heartbreaking and serious. Dangerous. Devastating. Read them with an open mind, and wonder if your son or daughter could ever be the writer. Be there for your kids. They need you!

Each of these letters required follow-up, sometimes with a return note, a quick meeting, or, in more serious cases, a referral to a counselor or a meeting with parents.

I've chosen to start with 'anxiety' because it has become such a common part of our kids' worlds. More children are diagnosed and treated for anxiety now than ever before. And many suffer without help. Here are some of their stories.

Dear Mr. Landes,

I have been having a problem. I have anxiety, but I don't know why I have it. Like, when I'm at school, I feel horrible, but when I'm at home, I feel fine.

I went to the hospital for my heart and lungs, and they gave me pills to take home. I hate my problem. I wish they would find out what's wrong. I just don't know what to do.

~ A junior student

MEDICATION, WHAT A RELIEF

Mr. Landes,

Yesterday, I went to a family youth therapist. I was diagnosed with depression, ADHD, and also anxiety. I'm supposed to be getting medication very soon! I'm relieved now that there's a solution, but I'm ashamed that my dad has pushed me to this limit.

~ A freshman student

ORCHESTRA EMBARRASSMENT

Dear Mr. Landes,

First off, I miss your class so very much!

Ok, so this month hasn't been my month, but I have kept up my positive attitude until today. Today, I had to play my orchestra playing test. I was super prepared but nervous.

I got into my teacher's office and had a panic attack, and everything started to fall apart. Randomly, my strings went out of tune, my bow started to catch, my hands started to shake, and my heart was going a mile a minute.

I was not prepared for a panic attack. I went to read the music, and I couldn't. It looked like gibberish, just ink on the page. What I read daily, and is normally common knowledge to me, was utter BS.

I had no clue what it said.

It was obvious that my teacher was irritated, which only made it 100% X worse, because no matter how hard I try, I can never impress him, and that's all I wanted.

I did terrible, and I truly was wretched. When I play, I am not half as bad when he isn't watching only me. I felt horrible walking out of his office, ashamed of what I had done/performed, and upset with how freaked out I was and how I had let it all fall apart. I am breaking out over how ashamed he must be of me.

I walked out of his office and almost lost it. But I stayed composed until he called out the seating/placing chart, and I was last. I knew that was going to happen, but from the self-loathing to the embarrassment, I couldn't help but let the tears just silently roll down my face as we went through some scales.

The worst part was looking into my teacher's eyes while mine were filled with tears. I knew it was my fault, and I felt so guilty that it all just overtook me.

All I want is to be the student, the musician, and the help that my teachers need, because everything else, I just screw up. I can't even do any of that right! He must be so ashamed and aggravated, and how selfish I was to cry and feel bad. It would be nice, for once, not to be bad at all the things I love!

~ A junior band student

CHAPTER

8

Death

One of the most heartbreaking things our kids deal with is the death of friends, parents, grandparents, or even pets. They don't have the life experience yet to handle the big emotions that often come with the death of a loved one, and their letters show how much they need our support in these times.

GRANDMA DIED

Dear Mr. Landes,

I am sad because I have been sick for a week. I have been having problems with my dad's side of the family, but I let out all of my emotions on Friday. Things are starting to get better. Sunday morning, my great-grandma Jennie passed away in her sleep. And the sad part is, she didn't remember who I was. But when I was little, we were close. Yesterday, I carried a blanket that she had made for me around with me all day. I miss her a lot. I am trying so hard not to cry right now. The weekend was emotional and bad. But inside, I am dying. Thank you for listening.

~ A sophomore student

SAD BECAUSE OF DEATHS

Dear Mr. Landes,

Today, when you were talking about somebody dying, I almost started crying for no reason. I think I was thinking about my Labrador dying when I was at school, and when my great-grandpa died in front of my older sister, and my great-grandma died in her sleep of a heart attack in this hospital, just like my great-grandpa did.

I really wanted to cry because I missed my great-grandparents, but I really missed my lab, who I took care of and who I cared for, the one who cheered me up when I was down. She was only about a year old. She died of parvo. She died because my dad was too lazy to get her fixed. The dog's name was Sunshine. She was the bestest good dog ever. I miss her and my grandparents.

I just wanted to tell you that I almost cried in class because I felt bad that my dog died. No other dog can fill the hole in my heart where my old lab used to be.

~ A freshman student

P.S. Today I have been quiet for some odd reason. Until Larry made me laugh hard when I was almost crying. He is a really good friend. If you see me put on my sunglasses, it usually indicates I am tired, or in a bad mood, or something is up!

TOO MANY DEATHS TO CANCER

Dear Mr. Landes,

The past few days, since the 16th, have been hard on me because my mom's uncle, my great-uncle, who lives in Montana, passed away. About a month and a half ago, we found out he was diagnosed with cancer. It was incurable and we didn't know how much longer he was going to live. It is kind of in the genes to pass away before the age of sixty for the guys on that side of the family. Just like his dad died because he was a smoker and an alcoholic. My papa, Uncle Bill's brother, is also a hard smoker. That's how Bill got cancer, because they have both been smokers since the age of thirteen.

It was an emotional roller coaster the morning we found out. The night before, my mom was talking to Kay, his wife, and wanted to talk to Jeff, but he was too tired and said he would call the next day. That morning, we got a call that he had died in his sleep. My mom was most hurt, but of course, seeing her cry made me cry. People are telling me he is going to a better place, but it's just hard to take that in. I'm also scared because my papa is still smoking A LOT and can't stop. I hate to think like this, but he's next, real soon. I'm closer to my papa, and when he passes, it will hurt me harder than my Uncle Jeff's passing. I couldn't tell this to you face-to-face because I would probably cry, and I don't want to cry anymore.

~ A freshman student

I CRY

I cry sometimes,
and don't know exactly why.
Because when I'm alone at night,
I feel like no one's by my side.
Whether awake or asleep,
beyond belief, it still
affects me three years later.
I always used to say, I have her,
but she broke up my family back in 05.
But four years later,
in 2009, my first stepdad, via suicide.
I've always asked why,
As tears filled my eyes,
because I never wished death to her at all.
I felt like God had forsaken me,
but I still believe because, you see,
I lost my grandma October 1, 2009 to brain cancer.
That night and summer, I was suicidal.

DEAR MR. LANDES

I told two people—won't name names.
But I believe they saved me.
Every year since then, I've always felt the pain,
again at this time of year.
But this year, I've wondered what
it would be like to believe.
I fear that death is around the corner,
about to take me and most of my family.
I'm trying my best to help my friend,
but most of the time, I feel like I'm failing.

~ A sophomore student

This is something I hope you like, and that I should've written a while ago.

CHAPTER

9

Little Things That Are Big Things

For teenagers, even the little everyday things can be big things. Their hormones and emotions run high, and things that seem relatively unimportant to most adults can be dramatic issues to our kids. While their lack of maturity can test our patience, they need us to demonstrate the calmness they crave and guide them in how to cope with these small problems as they arise.

A BAD WEEK

Dear Mr. Landes,

I have had a really bad week. I got sick, and I'm falling behind in my classes. I got grounded, and I have been fighting with my mom. I missed my bus this morning. Last night, I got jumped, but that's not bugging me, and I don't care about it. I'm just tired and I'm ready to give up!

~ A junior student

A FEVER

Dear Mr. Landes,

I have been running a fever, and I can't talk. My throat is really sore. I didn't come to school yesterday. I was running a 101 degree fever yesterday, and I still don't feel good.

~ A freshman student

PHONE TAKEN AWAY

Dear Mr. Landes,

I am having problems at home again. I am so sick and tired of my mom. She is always upset and never happy. So, she takes everything out on me. She always tries to find some reason to take my phone away. I just got my phone back three days ago, and she took it away this morning. I hate living there. I am so done with her.

~ A junior student

ANOTHER CRUDDY DAY

Dear Mr. Landes,

I think I'm just having a cruddy day all over again. Yesterday, my old friends were always bashing on me, and they are always pushing me into things. So, I guess they aren't really my friends.

Then, this guy called me fat and told me I looked horrible today. And on top of it all, I can't stop thinking about this girl I really like. And I know it's kind of pathetic, but I just can't stop thinking about her, only because she has made such a huge impact in my life. But I think she hates me!

So yeah, that's all.

Thanks for caring!

~ A freshman student

FEELING OF NOT SPECIAL

Dear Mr. Landes,

    The "To this day project" almost made me cry for the right reason. I really liked the video. If you want to check up on me and call me, I will give you my phone number at the bottom. At times, I have a major breakdown. Certain times, I've had the thoughts, "I'm not loved," "I'm not that special," and "I'm not as special as my older siblings." At times, I hate feeling like this. I have had my mom back me into a corner and yell at me. Certain things still linger with me on what has happened in my life.

~ A freshman student

HOW I AM FEELING

Dear Mr. Landes,

    I would ask of you to ask me how I am, and if I say I am fine, tell me 'Really?' and just ask me what is going on and how I am really feeling. Every day, there is something going on with me. Almost every day, I want to go home and cry. I have had many people hurt me. I have had thoughts of killing myself. Those people who get to me cause me really bad stress. Anyone I know doesn't know how to make me feel good about myself, but you make me feel good.

~ A freshman student

P.S. You will know when I am having a bad day because I will hardly smile or talk.

HAVE A GREAT WEEKEND

Dear Mr. Landes,
   Have a great weekend, Mr. Landes!
   I figured since everyone gives you notes about their problems, you needed an upbeat note!

~ A senior student

A BRIGHTENED DAY

Dear Mr. Landes,
   Life is really hard right now for me. My grandmother just died, and my boyfriend just broke up with me. I've been preparing for CMEA this Saturday and our smart chamber concert this Friday for months, practicing for months. And I recently found out my grandmother's funeral is this Saturday. And I can't make it to either of these events. It's just very difficult for me.
   But you just made my day by telling me you really like my smile and attitude, and your class always brightens my day! I just wanted to thank you!

~ A sophomore student

ANNOYING FRESHMEN

Dear Mr. Landes,
   I just wanted to let you know that you have to be the best English teacher I've ever had. What will make you even better is, don't let these immature freshmen keep you from what you do best, and that is motivating and inspiring students. I know they are annoying, but they'll be sorry one day.
   God's got his eyes on everyone!

~ A junior student

CHAPTER

10

Family Relationships

Many of my students ask the same questions. Why don't my parents want to be around me? What do I have to do to gain their approval? How much money would I have to pay for them to want to be with me?

Challenge: Do our children know that we love them? Have we told them? Have we hugged them lately?

If you are in a broken relationship, do you still desire to see your children? Do they know that?

If you are a parent who is using your kids as pawns or bargaining chips, know that you are hurting everyone. The children, your children's parent, and yourself! What do you tell your children about their parent who is no longer around? Do you attempt to make things better, or are you actually making it worse because of the pain that has been caused you?

ARGUING

Dear Mr. Landes,

I don't know how to really handle this. My family has been having some family drama. It's with my Nana and one of my aunts. They have been fighting a lot lately. I have a little cousin who looks up to me a lot.

Well, on Wednesday afternoon, she called, crying. She told me my Nana and my Tia (aunt) were arguing, and I could hear them in the background. I felt so bad, Mr. Landes, for my little cousin, and I didn't know what to tell her or how to help her. I just told her to go upstairs and lock herself in the bedroom. So, she did, and I stayed on the phone with her. Then, my Nana called me, crying and telling me what had happened and how she felt. Then, my aunt calls me to tell me how she feels. I'm caught in the middle. But to me, they are adults and they should know better. The person I care most for is my little cousin. She's been through so much in her life. Her mom can't take care of her, so my Nana does. I want to be able to help out my little cousin. I want her to feel that she does have someone in her life. Sometimes, I think she thinks that I don't love her, and I don't want her to feel that way about me. Then, to top all of that off, my great-grandmother is in the hospital. She had a knee replacement, and she's not doing well in recovery. I don't understand how people can be so selfish, and I think my Nana and aunt are selfish because how can they be fighting at a time like this?

~ Anonymous letter

CAUGHT IN THE MIDDLE

Dear Mr. Landes,

My mom and my older brother keep fighting, and I get pulled into it, and then I get yelled at if I don't agree with my mother. But sometimes, she's wrong. So, I get yelled at for saying my mind sometimes.

It's hard for me to talk about what's wrong or what's going on, so I write it down, but that's hard, too. But I feel like I can trust you, and that's a hard thing for me to do.

~ A junior student

NEVER GOOD ENOUGH

Dear Mr. Landes,

    I feel, some of the time, that I'm a disappointment to my parents. It's not good to feel like that, but whatever I do, for me or for them, it's never good enough, especially with my dad because we have a rocky relationship. He could say the nicest thing, and I get mad. I could get a B on a math test and be proud of myself because I'm not good at it, and he will tell me, You could do better. If you do this all the time, it's like, whatever I do in my life, it's never good enough.

    For instance, maybe I become President, and they say you could do better. Then, with my family, it's like I'm that kid in every family that is just a huge disappointment to them, or a waste of breath. Sometimes, I feel that they only love me out of sympathy, or because I'm a bad kid and they feel sorry for me. My parents and I fight constantly. Some of the time, I feel like they insult me because of my weight.

    Sometimes, I feel like I could die right now and nobody would notice, except for my parents. For a while, I keep it all bottled up, but I don't know why. I don't feel like I'm pretty enough. I feel dumb because I've never done really good in school, and yet I have big dreams for myself. I want to be a vet, but I don't have the grades, and I get in a lot of trouble for that by my parents. Most of the time, I feel like I'm not worthy enough for them. They deserve better than what they have in me.

~ A sophomore student

LOVE ME FOR ME

Dear Mr. Landes,

I just cried for two hours, and I wrote this poem:

Love me for ME

I try to be the one you wanted.
I tried to be perfect, like the firstborn.

DEAR MR. LANDES

I'm sorry I'm not the one you wanted,
I didn't ask to be born.
I feel disgraced to be your daughter.
You are the one who created me.
If I am not the one you wanted, give me to foster care.

I don't want to be here any longer.
I don't want to be your daughter anymore.
You don't love me as much as your firstborn,
She was perfect, she was girly.
I'M SORRY! I'M DIFFERENT!
I hope another family loves me better than you.
I will be more loved,
They will accept my small mistakes.
You make them out as a big deal.
I'm sorry I forgot one simple f***ing thing.
Not like I am meaning to do this,
It would be probably be better if I wasn't alive.
I try my hardest to please you, but I am unable to.
You have made my life so messed up,
I WISH I HAD A DIFFERENT FAMILY.

I would be loved then.
When you yell at me for the simplest things,
I feel like you don't love me anymore.
I am doing everything wrong.
Yelling doesn't help anything.
Talking nicely goes,
Stop blaming me for everything.
I'm not my fault I have short-term memory loss.
I hate being here.
I'm not loved here.
When I cry you say, "Suck it up!"
I'm not afraid to cry, unlike you.

You turned me into this monster.
"He who does not know how to serve, cannot know how to command."
At times, I wished I was in a bottomless pit.
When I can't laugh, you can.
When I am crying, you are happy.
You think taking things away makes things better; it doesn't
I live for my protection and to keep you out of my business.
When I cry, I make myself physically sick.
You both fight all the time.
I'm not sure I can take this any longer.
For how sad I am, I could just yell.

I want a family who loves me.
I want a family who doesn't yell and fight.
I want a family who accepts my mistakes.
I want a family to accept ME for ME.
Only if I could tell them certain things.
I have very low self-esteem because of you.
I feel like an OUTSIDER,
I probably don't belong anywhere.
You probably wouldn't care if I died in the cold.
I have thoughts about such things.
I'm weak when I have to tell you things.
I'm weak when I have to ask you for things.
Don't ever compare me to the firstborn, you love her more than me.

~ A freshman student

ROCK BOTTOM

Dear Mr. Landes,
    Lately, my life has been a little rocky. Sometimes I find myself in positions where I can't dig myself out of. I don't know what to do anymore with my past experiences with drugs.
    I went to rehab about three years ago, and ever since, my mom has

been overprotective of me. I know she cares about me, but there comes a time in my life where I just need my space. I don't take my sister to school every morning, but a couple of days a week, I will. The other days, I just have no motivation to get out of my bed. I'm always working, which makes me wear myself out for school. Sometimes, I wish I could just hit my rock bottom so that I can just start over again.

I want to be successful in life. I want to be the person who stands out and people actually notice and like for who I am, and not for how much money I have, or if I have a car.

I don't know anymore, Mr. Landes...

When I walk into your room and you talk about all this relationship stuff, which does help me, I would kind of like to how to deal with at-home family problems. I don't want to get my parents involved. I just want to see if I can do it on my own, and I want your help because you are one of the best teachers in the world, and you've been through so many life experiences that can relate to mine.

I don't want you to think that I'm just a kid who walks in late to your class and just doesn't care because that's not it at all. I just have a lot of stress on me right now, and I want help from someone who knows what they are doing... and you are that guy!

~ A junior student

TAKEN ADVANTAGE OF

Dear Mr. Landes,

Well, my friend that I have known for almost eight years passed away yesterday. He had a heart attack from a heroin overdose. He was only sixteen.

And also, my brother is just so rude to me, literally. I do everything for him, such as getting his clothes ready every day, starting his showers, washing his car, cooking for him, and so much more, and all I do is get treated like crap. We got into an argument this morning because he lost his memory card, and he got mad and blamed it on me. I said, "I never had your memory card," and he says, "OK, you're grounded until you find it."

I think it is just so messed up. There is just so much going on right now. It's all adding up, and I can't take it anymore. It's so hard to focus on school and myself when I'm getting screamed at and accused of always taking care of him. He's my guardian because my mom passed away when I was five, and they won't let my dad have me. I do all of this for my brother. He is thirty-five.

~ A junior student

CHAPTER 11

Fathers

Fathers are a significant and heartbreaking theme in many of the letters I receive from my students. Absent fathers, abusive fathers, children missing their fathers, and those who have never known a father's love and protection. So many men don't know how to be fathers, and yet their role is so important in teaching their daughters how to be respected and treated by men, and teaching their sons how to be respectful, strong, and loving partners to women.

I realize I'm the father figure for many of my students.

I weep for children who wonder if they are loved. The bigger lesson—and one I've lived—is that withholding a father's love causes our children to question: if an earthly father fails to love us, how can a heavenly father love us? I can assure you, I've spent most of my life trying to figure this one out. Until my spiritual father stepped into my life, I had never known the love of a heavenly father. I knew him intellectually, but I didn't have the tools to know him emotionally.

I am now very confident that my heavenly father loves me with a ridiculous love! He died for me so that I can live. I am the apple of his eye! He watches over, protects, and provides for me.

My prayer is that some parent reading this tells their children that they love them, and that reconciliation begins today. Blessings on the parents who love their children, who show them that they love them, and that they have no doubt of the love of an earthly parent, because you are helping them develop the love of the Heavenly Father!

How does a child spell love? TIME!

I remember reading a story about fathers to my students. Instead of asking the students to answer the questions at the end of the story, I wanted my students to relate to the story. So, I asked the students to write a paragraph about their father, another paragraph about the perfect father, and then a paragraph about what kind of parent they were going to be.

I learned so much about their fathers and their relationships with them. One boy said, "I don't want to write about my dad!" I told him to just go on to what makes a perfect dad. He wrote, the perfect dad doesn't cuss at his kids, doesn't hit his kids, and is helpful to his kids. What kind of man do you think his father was?

I read about parents who had passed away, were absent, and about abusive parents!

One girl wrote that her dad pays $500.00 a month in child support, but she would give it all back just to have a relationship with him.

Some kids' fathers died before they were born. One of my boys revealed that his dad was murdered! There were so many tragic, lonely, very sad kids, needing a positive, encouraging, protective father figure in their lives.

Since I had struck a chord and am naturally curious, I wanted to learn about their mothers. So, I had them write a paragraph about their moms, then what the perfect mother would be, and finally, what they wanted to ask their mothers, but were afraid to ask.

I am happy to say that most of my students were very happy and thankful for their mothers. Several of my students wanted to know why their mothers stayed with men who were abusive to them or didn't help.

One boy, I remember, had a simple question: "Is she proud of me?" I wasn't sure about this boy's past, but I assumed he struggled with grades or had addictions. He wondered a question many of us wonder. Are you proud of me?

One day, I gave my students a writing assignment to write about the impossible dream and the steps needed to accomplish this dream.

This student's paper ripped my heart out and is probably one of the saddest papers I've ever read in sixteen years of teaching. This paper was written by one of my junior girls, seventeen years old.

A DAUGHTER'S IMPOSSIBLE DREAM

Dear Mr. Landes,
 My impossible dream is for my dad to want me. I'm not sure exactly what I need to get there. I guess I need to become the daughter he wants, and I've got to learn what will make him want me around. I'm not sure this would need money, but if it would, and I had $1000, I would help him with some things he needs to pay. I would buy him anything he wants, and maybe then he'll love me enough to want me around. My dream has been impossible since I have been a little girl. Not even praying or anything has helped. So, I'm not sure what I need to make my impossible dream possible.

~ A junior student

 I assured her that her dad would love her if he only knew her. She is beautiful, smart, and very talented. She would be my ideal daughter! I assured her that it wasn't her problem; it was her father's problem. He was the one missing out, but she is paying the price of pain... the violence of silence.

MOVING, I HATE TORNADOES

Dear Mr. Landes,
 Eleven months ago, my dad was laid off, and he has been looking for a job ever since.
 My grandparents help pay for soccer and clothing. My dad just came back from a two-day interview, and I think he's getting the job. That means we would have to move to Oklahoma.
 I don't want to leave all my friends and family. They don't want us to leave either. I'm scared that we will leave and have no family or friends in Oklahoma, and when I come back, I won't have any friends here, and I'll have to start all over again.

On top of that, I'm scared of tornadoes. I know there are storm cellars, but I'm still scared.

~ A freshman student

P.S. We wouldn't go until the end of the school year, so I wouldn't see my dad for the rest of the year, except for Christmas. That's about seven months or so. That's the longest we've ever been apart. I love California, and I don't want to leave my dad for that long either.

NOBODY CARES

Dear Mr. Landes,

My dad abandoned us.

I'm alone. I put on a fake smile at times just to fool everyone. I cry at times from all the pain. I can't handle it. It hurts too much. 24/7. My father is not with us anymore. He left me around the time when I was about three years old.

I know I should be over it by now, but I'm not OK anymore. I cut my stomach sometimes because I cry so much, and I can't take the pain anymore. I can't talk to my mom because she thinks I am stupid for thinking about my father all the time.

He never calls anymore. He has another family and takes care of them, but not us, because he doesn't care about us. It's too much for me to think about, but I can't stop. Knowing that my dad cares for another child who isn't even his biological child, but he has one that is, and he just ignores me.

It makes me wanna cry. Another reason I cry and cut is because I'm fat, ugly, worthless, and stupid. It's really pathetic how I have "friends" when there is nothing special about me. When I need a friend to talk to, no one is there. No one cares. I mean, why would they? I'm stupid, pathetic, worthless, ugly, fat, and a freak. I cut because I am used to the pain. It just doesn't affect me, because I'm so used to the pain that it doesn't hurt.

I wish I was gone. I've already tried to kill myself twice. I almost did last week. I tried overdosing on pills, but I couldn't. I wish I did, though.

It would be so much easier for me to die, because I won't have to put up with this anymore. I'm tired of everything. I'm tired of crying. I'm tired of being tired.

I just want someone to care and listen, so of course, there's no one. Thanks for listening, Mr. Landes. Thanks for caring.

~ A freshman student

DAD AGAIN

Mr. Landes,

It's my dad again. Last week I didn't hear from my dad. He called my brother to tell him he got his truck taken away, and my mom looked to see why, and well, we saw that my dad had posted bail.

He calls me to tell me he's working stuff out, and he wants to have lunch sometime this week or next week.

~ A junior student

DAD ISSUES

Dear Mr. Landes,

I decided to write you something, and well, I hope you enjoy.

I know Thanksgiving has already passed, but I want to thank you for the little and big things you've done. You've made a big difference in my life, just by listening to me and giving me good advice. You're honestly my favorite teacher because you don't just teach us English, but you teach us about life.

You've made me understand a lot of things better. Thank you for giving me advice about my dad. It has helped me so much. I did what you told me, not to expect anything from him, and I'm glad I didn't. Every once in a while, he calls, but when I try to call him, he often isn't there. My mom gets tired of this happening, so she called him to talk to him about it, and she got so mad that she hung up on him, and she doesn't want to know anything about him. It kind of hurts me to know that, because when we are done talking, I just want to talk to someone about all the stuff I don't understand where he's coming from.

Anyways, thank you so much for everything.

~ A junior student

WORTHLESS

Dear Mr. Landes,

So last night, I had my first nervous breakdown. The main reason of that happening is because I'm at the boiling point with my dad. My dad makes me feel so bad about myself, and no matter what I do or say to make him happy, it's never good enough for him. School is also causing this ache upon myself.

I feel so alone. I'm beginning to feel helpless and worthless again. My dad even called me an outcast recently. Trust me, after school, I really need some guidance.

~ A junior student

NICE BOY WITH FLAKY DAD

Dear Mr. Landes,

Okay, well, I have a friend who means the world to me. I recently just got to know him beyond his everyday positive attitude. It came to find out his dad left him, and he's always struggled. He's pretty much had to become a young parent for his little brothers and sisters. He is such a wonderful person, and he always reminds of how beautiful life is and to always thank God for the day he has given me. He always asks me, "How was your day," and he always expects the same answer because I was given a day to live and to be thankful, and for that I am very fortunate. He texted me on Friday night and told me he wanted his space from his family and everyone around him, which I understand. But what hurts me is how emotional he is. He's beating himself up and punishing himself because his dad is just a flake. He brings his hopes up for no reason. My friend is missing a huge part in life, and I understand, but I really want to help him. I've said all I could, but he's just crushed by the missing piece of life he needs.

~ A freshman student

YOU THINK YOU HAVE IT BAD

Dear Mr. Landes,

Most people who hear about my life story either get really awkward about it or feel bad for me. To me, these are both really funny and annoying reactions.

I started out in what I thought was a perfect family. It was me, my mom, and my dad, but at that time, it didn't matter. We were, in my mind, the perfect family.

Once I got a little older, I realized how much Mom and Dad really taught me.

My dad once put a hole in the wall in my sister's room, big enough for us to walk right through to the kitchen. He once got arrested for it, too.

Finally, my parents split up when I was five. My dad and I moved into his mother's house. From that point on, my mother's life started to go downhill. I now know that both of my parents did a lot of drugs when I was younger, but never past a certain extent.

When my parents split up, my mother quickly hooked up with another man, and they lived together. Together, they both started using crystal meth, which resulted in my mom losing her house and having to move into a cheap trailer house. My mom and this man ended up having a son together. My brother is nine now.

They got kicked out of the trailer house and moved into the man's father's house when he was in the hospital after suffering a stroke. This place was a dump in downtown Modesto. The place rarely had any electricity or running water. We'd have to walk across the street to the park just so we could use the restrooms.

Eventually, this man and my mom split up. He cleaned up his life and is now taking care of his son with his new girlfriend. My mom then found another man she could get high with.

She conceived two baby girls within less than three years. This man is now in jail, and I have no clue where my mother is. But frankly, I don't care. The only thing that worries me is the safety of those two little girls. When me and my dad moved into my grandma's house, she was living with a close friend of hers. They are life partners. I call them lesbians just to get a reaction from people. LOL But that's not really what they are. Just two older women who are fed up with men, so they decided to split up the house bills.

I went through a stage once where I couldn't accept my grandma's friend. I quickly got over it, though. She's just as much my grandma as my real one is.

My dad went through various jobs. We moved in and out of Grandma's house twice. We now live in our own house, right around the corner from my grandma, and my dad is now a truck driver.

Over the years, me and my dad have not had the best relationship. My dad's always been an aggressive guy. He was always getting in fights when he was younger, and even some recently. I wouldn't call him an abusive father, because from what I see on TV, those types of fathers will beat their kids every day, and they are covered with bruises and stuff.

My dad is just mean. He's slapped me around and stuff, but again, I guess that isn't that bad. We've gotten worse, though. There's been times where I've been punched or kicked or had things thrown at me, but it could be a lot worse. He calls me a lot of names, too, like the b word and even worse. He'll call me retarded and stupid and say that I'm going to end up just like my mother if I make a little mistake or something. He hardly cares what I do at school, either.

I got an award last year, and he didn't want to go watch me get it, saying, "The only things I want to have to go watch are your soccer games and your high school graduation!" He was so bad when I played soccer. Constantly criticizing me and yelling at me. Finally, I quit, and he acts as if I'm a disappointment because of that, even when I bring home straight A's. I hate my father! He is immature and blames everyone else for his problems, just like my mother. But like he always says, at least he stayed, unlike her.

I never see my siblings, but I try to stay in touch with my sister. She's one of the only people I know who can fully understand me and my life.

Most of my family treats me like I'm three and too immature to understand anything, and that I'll never be able to succeed in life. But I don't care, really, what they or anyone else thinks of me. I'd rather they didn't think about me at all.

Well, that's my life, I guess. I'm sure there are a bunch of details I left out, but this is already long enough as it is!

~ A sophomore student

NO EMOTION DAD

Dear Mr. Landes,

Today, I saw my dad, and I told him how I felt, and how it hurt that I never see him. I was crying really bad, and he just stood there looking at me, and I just wanted to go home!

~ A junior student

END THE DRAMA

Mr. Landes,

My mom is going to sign some papers so my dad gets served with them, and he will have to go to court, and if he doesn't show, he will have a warrant out for him. I just want all of the drama to end and my dad to get what he deserves, finally.

~ A sophomore student

And just when it seems like all the dads in the world are useless, there's these:

LATE HOMEWORK

Dear Mr. Landes,

This is Mr... writing to ask you to please give her a significantly reduced grade for the paper she is turning in today.

We found out that she did not write the paper due to her just being lazy, which we do not condone. She is a great kid, as well as a straight-A student, so this was a surprise to us.

Her mom and I believe that to give her full credit will send the wrong message to her about how life in the real world is.

We expect her to complete all of her work on time, so there is no excuse for the late paper. In fact, we are very unhappy about the significant lack of homework she has in any of her classes. She has very little to no homework in school at all, which is also teaching her that life is easy, which I'm sure you know that it isn't.

Thanks for your time, and please reply to my email to acknowledge that she gave this to you along with her paper.

Thank you,
~ A freshman student's dad

A FATHER'S LOVE

Dear Mr. Landes,

Since you're talking about Fathers today, it made me think of a song that you may want to show your next class, or even this one. It's called *Love Without End, Amen*.

My boyfriend used to think his father didn't love him. I showed him this song, and it made him cry when he realized his dad did love him.

I don't know. It's just a suggestion. You can find this song on You Tube. Here are some lyrics:

> "Let me tell you a secret about a Father's love, a secret that my daddy said was just between us. Daddies don't just love their children every now and then, it's a love without end, amen."

That's why it reminded me about fathers. The whole song is about fathers.

P.S. It might change how some of us students that don't think our fathers love us really do!

~ A junior student

CHAPTER

12

Friendship

Learning the art of navigating friendships is one of the biggest challenges our teens face on a daily basis, and in our world of online social media, it's a bigger challenge than ever. Cyberbullying, a culture of saying hurtful things behind the safety of a screen, and people who prey on the weak, pretending to be friends, makes the world a much less reliable and stable place than we knew as teens.

They need our help in learning to identify true friends, how to be a good friend to others, how to spot a fake, and what to do about it, how to manage jealousy, disappointment, arguments, love, and all the rest that comes with friendships.

FRIENDSHIP PROBLEMS

Dear Mr. Landes,

Well, I'm grounded again, but that's not what is bothering me. My friend didn't come down yesterday, and I was really excited to see him because I hadn't seen him in, like, almost two months. But the good thing is that he is coming around the 24th.

But my other friend and I got into a big fight, and we're not talking. Today is his birthday, also, but we've been through a lot, and he has hurt me so much in the past years, I couldn't take it anymore.

He has been my best friend, and I stood by his side when everyone else left him, even though he hurt me emotionally every day. I know this fight, and now us not talking is good for me because I don't have to deal with his immature shit anymore. But it kind of hurts walking around, seeing him, and acting like I don't know him and don't care, but I think it's best.

~ A junior student

TWEETS

Dear Mr. Landes,

So, I guess I just had a bad weekend. For about a month, my friend and I have been fighting about little things, I guess. So yesterday, on Twitter, I saw she had a second account, and I went to the last time she had posted and read some of her posts. I started scrolling, and I start to see things that are about me. It's bad! And she's tweeting things like, I make her feel bad and that she's wasted her time just hanging out with me. And a bunch of other horrible things.

So, I'm just angry. Like, about everything!

Thanks for caring!

~ A sophomore student

I NEED ANSWERS

Dear Mr. Landes,

I was wondering if you could talk to one of your students for me and just ask him why? And also, what does he want from me?

I want to know, and it is killing me that we can't have a conversation, and it seems he doesn't even want to talk to me anymore.

So, if you could talk to him, that would be helpful. Thank you.

I think he will listen to you more than my friends because he doesn't always believe what they say, or what I say!

Thank you

~ A junior student

CHAPTER 13

Young Love and First Relationships

I think this is what we all think of most when we think about teens—the raging hormones and passionate first love experiences. And while these things are certainly true, they are highly stressful events for our kids as they learn to navigate dating, sex, conflict, jealousy, and all the other fun stuff that comes with relationships.

We need to be there for our kids, to help them learn how to be a good partner and friend. We need to listen without inserting our fears and judgments, and offer advice without holding on too tight. Mostly, we need to model good relationships for our kids so they know what it looks like, how to deal with problems, and how to feel good about themselves within a partnership.

These are some of my favorite letters—funny, beautiful, and heartbreaking in their innocence. We think our teens know so much, but these letters show how much they still have to learn—often the hard way.

A STONE HEART

Dear Mr. Landes,

A Stone Heart:

    I'm glad you asked me how I was doing, Landes, because really, I am hurting inside.
    I feel like my heart has turned to stone and that there is no way it can bleed anymore. I've been hurt really bad a lot of times, and I honestly don't know what to do about it.
    This is the third time my heart has been crushed, and this time I know it's the worst it's ever been. I know I'm a strong person, but I feel weak because she has attacked my ultimate weakness. My heart!
    She says she's sorry and she understands that what she did was really wrong, and no matter what, if I don't forgive her, she'll understand. But I do, and people say to me that she really doesn't care, especially because of what she did. I just can't help it. I believe she is sorry, but another part of me says maybe she is just saying that. There's more to say but I'd rather talk about it than write it out on paper.

PS. Can we just keep this between us?

~ A junior student

ALL I DO IS CRY

Dear Mr. Landes,

    I need someone to talk to right now, and you seem like just the person. I've been so sad lately. This guy I really like, I've known for a long time, we have gotten so close to each other, and I just like him so much, and he does, too, but he lives in Sunnyvale, a one-hour and thirty-minute drive away! It didn't really bother me until a few days ago, when I started getting attached. I think about him all the time and wonder when I might see him again. He said he won't be able to come down until Summer. IDK, I need some words of encouragement. All I do is cry, cry, cry.

~ A freshman student

TEENAGE LOVE

Dear Mr. Landes,

There is just a lot going on in my social life. My best guy friend and me are no longer friends because he is jealous of my ex-boyfriend, who I still have feelings for. He got mad at me and called me a bitch because I want to be with my ex. So, I told him I wanted nothing to do with him.

But my ex, well, we broke up last Thursday, and I still have feelings for him, and he has feelings for me. So, he says. We broke up because I was jealous, and he liked another girl, and he says he doesn't want to hurt me, and he's trying to figure out if he wants to commit to me or whatever.

The thing is, I can see my whole life with him. We have been together for four years, so he's kind of all I know, and I wanna be with him because I think I honestly do love him. But I don't know if I can trust him. But we're still together, it seems, because we have the same group of friends, we talk literally all day, and we're going on a date Friday.

I just don't know what to do. I'm scared and I don't want to get hurt.

~ Anonymous letter

My advice isn't always well-received. But she came back for more!

CONFLICTED

Dear Mr. Landes,

I think you should know who this is. He does not slow me down at all. If anything, he is my motivation. He keeps me going. Everyone has their own kind of motivation, and he is mine. He means a lot to me, and he's changed me for the better, and I thank him for that.

Ever since day one, people have been trying to tear us down, but we do not care. We are together for a reason, and nothing anybody says is going to change that.

I know you have my best interests in mind, but please just don't say stuff like that because it's not true.

We have been through a lot, and it has made us stronger. Little things like that (to me) are unnecessary and uncalled for. I would appreciate it if you could keep comments like that to yourself. I'm going through a lot right now, and I hate it when people judge me.

But one thing I want to know is, what to do about the conflict I have with my ex's girlfriend? It's not like it's his girlfriend, but I just have never liked her. She does stuff on purpose and she knows it. It just hecka irritates me, and at times I want to hit her so hard, and I'm never going to like her, but I don't know what to do.

Thank you,

~ A junior student

FIGURING OUT GIRLS

Dear Mr. Landes,

On Sunday, my friend told me she had done some things with her friends. I really got mad, but I didn't let her know. I was telling her she was better than that, and that started an argument. What really got me upset was that even though I was looking out for her, she was talking to me as if she hadn't done anything wrong.

I told her that if she thought it was OK to do those things, I'm just not going to care anymore. She really got mad about that. So, Monday, she wrote me a note, saying how much she loves me. I was talking to her that night, and I told her that we should just move on and forget about what had happened.

She agreed, but she still said that she was mad. To me, it felt as if she was mad because I cared about her. Later on that day, she wanted to apologize. I only apologized because I wanted to move on.

She then told me she likes me, but it doesn't seem like she really does. I'm always the bad guy when I go a day and I don't interact with her. She never shows effort in what she says.

I just don't understand her at all. All the little things I do for her appear unnoticed. She makes me want to give up. She makes me want to stop trying because I feel so unappreciated.

I've talked to her about this issue, but it seems like it's no use. If she keeps this up, I will stop and will start treating her like a friend rather than treating her as a girlfriend.

Thanks for listening,
~ A sophomore student

GOD SAID

Dear Mr. Landes,

Well, so far, the divorce between my parents has been really rough on me. I've had a really hard time accepting it. I've been missing school a lot because I go back and forth between my mom's and dad's house. My dad's car is broken down until tomorrow or Saturday. So, when I'm over there, I don't have a way to school. But my parents want me to do homeschool, so I may only be here at school for two or three more weeks.

But also, I don't know if you remember my friend from across town, he goes to my church. I've known him since I was little, and I was practically raised with him my whole life. But I've literally been in love with him for the past five years, and he knows, but he's very confused and likes to play too many games. He'll act like he likes me and flirts with me, but then the next day, he does the same thing with other girls. But we've been best friends for about three years now, and he's really close to me and my family. I think he's too caught up in playing games with girls' minds because girls can never figure him out. He's very insecure, and it makes him feel good to know that a lot of girls like him, so that's why he flirts with other girls so much.

But I think that if he waits too long to realize that God made us for each other, he's going to miss out because I'm not going to wait for him forever. But God speaks to me, and what God says goes, and God doesn't lie, and

I believe what he told me. About three or four years ago, God told me that this boy is for me, and what I pray in secret will be rewarded openly. And I believe that with all my heart. I know God will speak to him, too, but if he doesn't listen, then it's not going to work out. But so far, that's what's been bothering me. And I've been really hurting from it.

~ A junior student

HE MADE ME FEEL SPECIAL

Dear Mr. Landes,

    I have been depressed for a couple of days now because my boyfriend broke up with me. I could have helped him with what he is going through, but I guess he thought it would hurt our relationship. I could have been an emotional support for him, but I guess he didn't think of that. He was nicer than any of the other guys here. He made me feel special when I was in a bad mood and when I didn't feel right; he even would make me blush at the randomest moments. Not even one guy can make me blush the way he made me blush. It feels like I won't find a guy exactly like him.

    P.S. I was crying for two days straight. I even cried at school. Plus, I was having thoughts of cutting myself again. I have held my urge back as best as I can.

    Can you do me a favor and on Monday or Wednesday, can you please play "Stay Beautiful" by Taylor Swift?

~ A sophomore student

I CAN'T LIVE WITHOUT HIM

Hi Mr. Landes,

    I've been really sad lately for multiple reasons. I am sad because I <u>always</u> feel I'm not pretty or skinny enough. I am scared, though, that if I keep starving myself, I'll look even uglier because I'll only be a skeleton.

When I do eat, I have a condition called something like anorexia bloating, where my stomach is unused to eating, so it doesn't really know how to act. It will swell, and sometimes it can hurt me. It's very annoying because it makes me feel even bigger.

Also, I'm sad because my mom has some problems about he and I. She doesn't know we are together, but I really wish she did. And since she has <u>severe</u> anger and violence problems, I can't bring it up because I'm scared. To be completely honest, Mr. Landes, I truly love him with all of my broken heart. He is the only person who can turn the worst day of my life into the greatest day of all, just by smiling. I am with him about thirty-six hours a week and his family greatly approves of me. I <u>am</u> going to marry him, Mr. Landes. I really mean it. It may not make sense, but something about him and I being together forever make all the sad things about my past and present completely disappear. He is, without a doubt, my favorite person in the whole entire world. There is no way I could live without him. That's another reason that I'm sad, though. I'm terrified that he'll leave me. I just want to be the best girlfriend ever. I'm worried that he's unhappy with me. Anyway, he helps me with my problems, and he's always there for me. He is my 18th (I think) guy, and I <u>know</u> he's what I've been waiting for. Sorry to write such random letter, but these are the main things on my mind. Thank you!

~ A freshman student

IS IT LOVE

Dear Mr. Landes,

Good morning. Well, I have a boyfriend. You know, the guy that none of my friends like. By the way, we fought yesterday, but yeah, there is this guy I've been talking to, and we met up and hung out for the first time on Sunday with my friend. We also hung out yesterday, and today, this morning. And by the way, he is a complete dork, and he was really sweet. He said I have a really pretty smile, and he was sweeping my bangs away from my face. It's hard for me to like someone, but at the same time, I'm scared to do anything. I'm so mixed up about this. I don't know what to do, plus I don't know if he's this sweet to other girls, even though he says he isn't. He also wanted me to hang with him after school, but I can't. I'll talk to you soon, Mr. Landes.

~ A junior student

MAN WHORE

Dear Mr. Landes,

The basic summary of why I was unnerved yesterday is because I broke up with my girlfriend of one year and four months because she cheated on me, countless times. I started dating this other girl. We have a lot in common, and then a week later, she broke it off with me and told me she didn't want a boyfriend.

I was fine with that because she had explained to me that if she was with me, she wanted to be with her ex, and when she was with him, she wanted to be with me. Her ex doesn't like her anymore than just being friends, and my other friend has liked her for about a year and a half now. I didn't know that until afterwards, though.

But anyway, I developed a crush on another girl, and I explained to my ex, and she seemed fine with it. So, yesterday, when I'm with this new girl, my ex has been crying for days and days. Five people hate me and think I'm a man whore. My ex and I are just friends.

PS. My friend confessed to liking her for so long last night and only talked about how much she likes me. Oh, and me and this new girl broke up one week ago today.

Do you think I'm right?
My thoughts are that she only wants what she can't have.

~ A junior student

OUT OF CONTROL

Dear Mr. Landes,

A Poem:

Out of Control

Passion, happiness, laughter, excitement—all these amazing sensations.
Invincibility, an endless smile, a joyous laugh—all from just you.
It feels so wrong, but yet so right to be by your side,
These memories inside swirling, twirling, unwilling to reside in the corner of my mind,
Leaving me restless and incomplete.
Ah, to close my eyes, and let time fly by because there is so much to gain,
by forgetting these dreams, which are driving me insane.
Unfocused, unclear, out of control, my world spinning, spinning, spinning,
my sanity flying through the door. My reason, my logic, oh, it's tragic,
like fine sand running through my hands, I'm losing my mind.

~ A junior student in love

CAN YOU HEAR ME NOW

Dear Mr. Landes,

So, I haven't been doing very well lately. I really feel like nobody cares to even listen to me.

I know my boyfriend says he does, and I know he tries. But I feel like I need to yell in order for him to hear me. He gets really distracted easily. But I just feel like he isn't really paying attention.

He sometimes listens when he plays video games, but I like making eye contact when we talk. I don't think he's really listening when he's playing a game, you know?

And life has been so stressful. So far, I've lost my house, so I'm homeless now. I've sort of been bouncing around. First, I stayed with my boyfriend, but I had to leave when his dad came home from overseas. Then, I went with my mom to her friend's house. Last night I was at another friend's house. It's really hard figuring out how to get to school. My mom can barely walk, so she's out of a job, and we're waiting for her disability to come in so we can rent an apartment.

I've also been struggling with anxiety and depression. I haven't cut for a long time, and it's getting really hard, and it's so hard for me to talk to my boyfriend. I want to feel like he will listen to me. I don't feel like he would understand either. We always used to talk about things, and it always used to make me feel better. But now that we've been together so long, I don't think he really remembers how it used to be.

I just really need somebody right now, and it's hard to talk about my feelings to others. I always get, "You're too depressing!" and "That sucks!" The only really good advice I receive is from another friend, but I 'm scared I bug him too much. I know he's having a hard time right now, too. I just don't know what to do anymore!

~ A junior student

VERTIGO

Vertigo

    I feel like my emotions are in this constant state of Vertigo.

    These feelings I experience are so vast that they never quite touch down in one place. My body tremors with bruised depression and sun-kissed joy.

    All of this dazed stumbling revolves around the question of "Who am I?" This Vertigo is a twisted, blackened form of my reality.

    Am I the broken body that he left me with, or am I the striving young woman I pretend to be? I twist and turn in the debatable relevancy of my life to his.

~ A senior student

CHAPTER

14

Sex and Teen Pregnancy

Sometimes, those first relationships get a little too real! The deep feelings and confusion that make young love so enchanting can also come with hard choices, life-changing consequences, and a great need for adult support, love, and assistance.

Model healthy relationships for your kids. Have the hard conversations. Be open, approachable, and honest when it comes to discussing sex. Try to stick to the facts and keep your protective emotions out of it (hard to do!). Most of all, love your kids, no matter what, without judgment and anger. That way, if they do have a serious problem, they will know you are a safe person to go to for help. These issues are too big for our kids to deal with alone.

SHOULD I GIVE IT UP

Dear Mr. Landes,

I have no one else I can go to for this. Everyone else will just depress me about this.

I really want to be with this boy more than anything. But he just wants a quicky! He wants me to lose my virginity to him. I made him promise he won't leave me afterward. He promised. I really don't know if I can trust him with that. He's hurt me before. Last school year, in fact. 8th grade. We met, and he said he liked me. I told him I liked him, too. He said he had a girlfriend, though. I was like, let's just be friends then, I don't want to mess up anything. And it's true. I didn't. He started having really bad problems with her and came to me for help. I hated seeing him hurt. He eventually started coming over to my house. He ended up cheating on her with me. Never sex, though. Just making out. Then last June, he broke my heart.

I found out from her MySpace that they were back together again. They had broken up for a while. He didn't talk to me until Christmas break of Freshman year. I told him I was suicidal. I was in such depression. I tried killing myself three times over the summer.

He made a promise that he would never hurt me again like that. They broke up after their anniversary. We've been basically BFF (Best friends forever) ever since. I'm still in love with him. I've never stopped and I never will. I have major trust issues because of him. I mean, I told him everything about me. He said he loved me and took it back. Now, he says he cares for me and loves me. WELL, IF THAT'S TRUE, why doesn't he ask me to be his girlfriend, you know? I'm trusting him until he proves me wrong.

I just need to know if I'm making the right choice and if I should give him my virginity? I just want to see him happy. I'm just scared of what might happen.

~ A very confused little girl

I THINK I'M PREGNANT

Dear Mr. Landes,

So yet again, I've got some terrible news. I'm pretty sure that I'm pregnant. I don't really have anyone that I can trust with this, or even anyone that can help me.

My boyfriend and I went to his house on Saturday, and we had sex with a condom, but it broke very early into intercourse.

I'm very scared. My parents will kick me out if I am pregnant.

My boyfriend will stay by my side if I am, but neither of us deserves this stress so early in our lives. I'm not exactly sure who I should be going to about this situation, but no matter what happens, my parents CANNOT find out!

I did lots of research on abortions and the laws of California about abortion. I'm very scared.

I am aware that I can take a pill within 110 hours of intercourse, and I'm running out of time.

What should I do? I'm so scared. I have a therapist, and she said anything I tell her stays confidential, but can I really believe her? Please help me!

~ A junior student

PREGNANT

Dear Mr. Landes,

If I was to be pregnant and had no one else that can help me, would you be willing to give me some help? There's a possibility that I am, and I haven't told anyone, and I can't let anyone know!

~ A junior student

I need some advice, ASAP!!

MY PARENTS WILL KICK ME OUT

Dear Mr. Landes,

Please help me. I think I might be pregnant, and nobody can know, especially my parents. If they find out, they will kick me out!

This statement, 'my parents will kick me out of the house if they find out I'm pregnant,' angers me on so many different levels.

If we don't step up to take care of these children, if we don't stop kicking our kids out of the house because they have disappointed us, if we don't come up with a solution, we are making it worse for everyone.

I remember sitting in church one day, and the preacher said, "There are no illegitimate children, but there are plenty of illegitimate parents."

Why? Why would you kick your child out of the house because they are pregnant? Smoked? Got drunk? Etc. I believe some kind of discipline should be established, but kicking them out of the house? Shouldn't we be talking to our children? Shouldn't we be involved in their lives? Shouldn't we be a listening ear? Shouldn't we be loving arms to run to when they have fallen?

As long as we react with pride and shame, we will drive our hurting, helpless people away from the place that should be the safest, most comforting place to go.

I ask you, what would you do?

CHAPTER 15

Coming Out

Love is a many-splendored thing. Many of us adults were raised to believe that homosexuality was wrong. And many of us won't change very fast. And yet, the world has changed, and coming out as gay, lesbian, queer, and trans has become a more open and common occurrence, although one still fraught with worry and stress.

Finding our voices is one of the hardest things for our kids to do, but once they do, it becomes very powerful. Hopefully, you can be compassionate, understanding, and sympathetic to the child who feels alone and lost. Accepting your child for who they are will bring you both great peace to move forward.

Dear Mr. Landes,

Here is my story. In life, my most shocking experience was getting to know and realizing my chances in life. All my life, I've never made choices by myself, and I never had to defend myself. My life was being run by my family.

Well, at age 12, my siblings and I were put into foster care. We were together a few months before they separated us into different foster homes.

I was young, but I knew I wasn't home. I was picked on by people, and I didn't know how to defend myself. I had to adapt to a whole new environment alone. And on the other side, I was beginning to realize more about my own sexuality. I became scared, lost, and lonely. I was being moved from foster home to foster home. By the fourth foster home, I became mad that I liked guys. And I didn't want people not liking me because of that.

My foster mom used to beat on my foster sister, and before she could get to me, I spoke up for myself, and I had to be moved out of that home. For the first time in my life, I realized I no longer had my mom, brothers, or sisters to protect me, and I had to protect myself or I would end up getting hurt.

By the end of 2007, I had been in five foster homes and two group homes in a year. It's not that I was a bad kid, but I had problems I was trying to cope with, and people didn't respect that.

I had come out with my sexuality, and I was put into an LGBT group home. It taught me more about myself, and it opened up my outlook on life. I was a young, independent, gay, African-American male, and I would only become better in time and stronger the more struggles I overcame. And I am ready to do anything to get a career and a life better than what I've been living. All I need is my education.

Thank you for listening.

~ A junior student

IT JUST BREAKS MY HEART

Dear Mr. Landes,

"It just breaks my heart!" is a common quote from my mom. I told my mom that my friend, Gary, is gay. "Oh, that breaks my heart," she said. I told my mom that a guy I liked was bisexual. "Oh, that just breaks my heart." I came out to my mom, telling her I was bisexual. "Oh, it just breaks my heart." My cousin came out this month. "Oh, it breaks my heart."

Does it? Does it really? It pains you that my first love was a girl, Mom? That my cousin is finally happy and able to tell our family that he's going to marry the man he loves? What about me, Mom? You don't think it hurts me, Mom? That if I decided the person I love and want to be with forever was a woman, I wouldn't have your support?

It does break my heart that little kids hold signs saying "God hates fags!" Sorry, ma, I no longer care that love just breaks your heart.

~ A sophomore student

CHAPTER

16

Depression

Depression is far from uncommon in teens. They seem to carry the weight of the world more heavily than most adults, probably because they don't have the life experience, the tools, or the mature understanding to deal with many of the challenges they face.

Depression in teens can look like irritability, difficulty concentrating, lack of motivation, laziness (actually fatigue or low energy), and poor school performance, all behaviors that are easy to misinterpret and can make us frustrated as parents and teachers. Other signs of depression could include weight changes (increase or decrease), changes in sleep patterns, risk-taking, social withdrawal, and even physical complaints.

Stay approachable, listen without judgment, and offer your unconditional support. Depression is hard enough without an angry parent or teacher pushing you to 'snap out of it.'

If your child's depression seems severe or they are having suicidal thoughts or self-harming, seek professional help.

TURNING THINGS AROUND

Dear Mr. Landes,

    I want to thank you. Thank you for just being the beautiful, caring person you are. I thank God that I had you as a teacher. Some students may not have enjoyed your class, but I personally loved your class. Not only did you teach and prepare us for the real world, but you taught us how to learn from our mistakes and that life is not easy. You showed us how we can make ourselves stronger.

I have to be honest, the first day I walked into your classroom, I was not a happy person. I was always so sad. I was depressed and lonely. I was just so tired and done with life. It was hard for me to find reasons to live. My life was getting worse and worse as time went by. Every day, I would sit in my room planning ways to kill myself and thinking about what to say in my suicide letter. I was in a horrible place, and your class truly changed my life!

No joke, Landes, your class helped me a lot. Like when you would give us those affirmations every week, and we would read them as a class. I would truly listen to the words and take them in. Also, when you would tell us stories about your life and the hard times you had. Especially the first time I opened up to you. It felt nice to know I had someone there for me.

Getting more and more into the year, during Winter break, my depression got so much worse. I continued to cry myself to sleep every night. I would cut almost every day. I just wanted to feel another pain to distract me from the pain I dealt with every day. I truly wanted to die. I could not handle things anymore. It was so hard.

I remember coming home one night, and I couldn't eat. I went into my room and started crying. I've never cried so hard in my life. I sat there looking at the fresh cuts I had just made in my hand, feeling my hand sting, and seeing the blood dripping from different places. I wanted to kill myself so badly that night. I can't explain how hard I was crying. I remember looking over at my binder, and I decided to read some papers you gave us.

After reading the papers, I told myself, "One more minute, one more hour, one more day!" I would constantly tell myself that. Things started to change, school-wise. It got a little bad. I became so lazy. I would not try anymore. I won't even try with my looks anymore. I saw it as I had stopped trying to live.

You would tell me that I was slacking in your class and that I was lazy. I would just fake a smile and laugh because you know what, I didn't care. I really did not give a fuck! About anything at all. Not school, not myself, not anything. I was just done! I figured, I'm going to end things anyway, so what's the point of trying anymore?

I would lie to you by saying I was going to give you my assignments soon, because I didn't want you to see me as a slacker or as a failure, even though I was. I couldn't really change anything at this point. It was the last week of school, after all.

Well, this summer, I left. I went to my aunt's house. I was there basically the whole summer. It gave me time to get away from my everyday life. I had time to think clearly and had a chance to be truly happy. Over there, I felt loved, wanted, and really accepted. I thought of ways to make my life at home better. How to fix things with my mom and her boyfriend. How to deal with the depression that I've had for the past three years. Wow! That's crazy, I think I've had this depression for the past three years.

Being over at my aunt's, I felt like I was my old self again. I was so incredibly happy over there. I would wake up excited to start the day. When I was depressed, I would have a hard time getting out of bed each morning. I didn't even want to start my day. Well, I was always happy, always smiling and laughing. My aunt became my best friend. I vented to her and told her how I had been feeling and how hurt I had been the past few years. She understood and was there for me!

So, what I'm saying is that my depression went away. I no longer feel the need to hurt myself, or cry at night, or be upset constantly. My relationship with my mom has gotten better. I have to say, coming home after those two and a half months was really hard for me. I think saying goodbye to my aunt was one of the hardest things I've ever had to do. I cried the whole first day I was back at home.

I've gotten used to being back. It's still hard not being with my aunt anymore. I'm just glad I don't sit in my room and cry and cut anymore. It feels so good to be happy. I feel so free! So FREE! Like, OMG! I haven't been truly happy in a very long time. It feels weird not being sad all the time, but it's amazing!

I cleaned out my old school bag and went through my binder and found ALL the papers you gave us... all of them... every single one! I smiled! I read them. I felt like a completely different person. I felt like I became stronger. Mr. Landes, I want to thank you deeply because you were honestly a big part of the reason I became stronger. Not only your class, papers, and videos, but you, as a person. You were there for me. I truly appreciate when you would pull me to the side and tell me how proud you were of me. God blessed me to have you as my teacher. He brought you to me to help me and help lead me to strength and happiness. I would also like to apologize for lying to you. Lying about my moods and the whole assignment thing.

Mr. Landes, please, please, don't ever change! You are an AMAZING man. I'm so happy and thankful I had you as a teacher. From now on, I want you to know that every time you see me smile and laugh, it is a REAL smile and laugh. That's me, really happy. I won't be faking it anymore, and you are a part of the reason why I'm happy. I'm going to keep all of the papers you gave us… FOREVER! I'll be visiting you, too. I'll talk to you if I ever need to talk to someone, because I know you'll be there.

Ha Ha Ha… I also have a confession. I would text you on holidays and wish you a Happy Thanksgiving or Merry Christmas. I would never sign my name, and you would say the same thing every single time. "Do you want to know what I think about people who don't sign their names? I think those people are cowards!"

Well, I honestly was a coward, but I'm not anymore. I've changed. Into a better and happier me! I want to thank you one last time for making that possible. Thank you deeply, Mr. Landes! Never change! I love you, and I'm going to miss seeing you every day in 5th period. I'll very much miss your smiling, laughing, joyfulness, and most of all, your singing! Understand, you are a huge part of my story!

~ Your sophomore female student
~ in ^{5}th period of the years 2012-2013

P.S. Sorry if the letter was confusing or scrambled… I was in the zone!! :)

HIDING THE PAIN

Dear Mr. Landes,

So, I went to the doctor yesterday, and the doctor told me that my depression is getting worse, that on a scale of one to ten, my depression is at eight and a half, and I can feel it coming on, sometimes. Even though I'm at school, I try not to show it, but like, around fifth period is when it shows up the most. Like, I sit there and I just want to cry. All my bad memories come back, and sometimes I tear up, but most of the time I don't because I don't want people to judge me.

~ A junior student

LIFE LESSONS

Dear Mr. Landes,

Throughout my time in ESS, I've learned a lot. To be completely honest, I did not learn academically. I have learned more life lessons than anything else. I've learned that giving up is not an option if I want to succeed. I want to give up a lot if I'm being honest, not because I'm a quitter, but because a lot of the time, I just don't want to be alive. I don't know if I'm a suicidal person. I just know I'm tired. I can't really give up on life, though. It would kill my parents, and I don't want to hurt them. I guess I really just want my high school life to be over already. I want to start my career in cosmetology already. I just want this part of my life to end already. I'm disappointed in my 2017-2018 self for digging such a deep academic hole. I've learned that no matter how much I don't want to be alive, I don't actually want to not be alive. I just have to get through the rest of this. I have to ground myself and I was really good at that at the beginning of this junior year, but then I fell into the biggest depressive episode I've ever experienced, and it's been really hard to get out. It's like the me that wants to live and succeed in life is fighting so hard to resurface, but I don't know why I haven't yet. I know I can do it, though. I know that much.

~ A freshman student

MORE HELP THAN YOU KNOW

Dear Mr. Landes,

    I've been having some problems lately. I struggle with depression and suicide. I'm on depression pills and used to go to counseling. Monday night, my boyfriend told his parents I was raped last May. They called and told my mom, but she doesn't believe me. She thinks I'm lying for attention. I've had a lot of family issues the past few years, but they're getting better.

    Other than that, my cousin passed away in December, and my Grandpa has been diagnosed with stage three colon cancer. Things are OK. I thought I would let you know. You know, your class and your optimistic outlook on life really helps, encourages, and inspires me daily. So, I'd like to thank you. You've been more of a help than you know!

Thank you.
~ A senior student

A LITTLE GIRL'S STRUGGLE WITH HER DEPRESSION

Dear Mr. Landes,

    I've always known I've had a different kind of sadness inside me ever since I was little. At first, I thought it was normal to feel the kind of sad that I feel. Granted, I've always felt everything incredibly deep – happiness, excitement, but the things I feel even deeper are love, loss, and sadness.

    When I was little, I used to get bullied a lot for the way I looked. Then, when I was in the first grade, my mom started to go away a lot, more specifically for thirty days at a time. That wasn't easy for me. It wasn't easy for anyone. But that was my mom, and I can't tell you how many times my six-to-eight-year-old self cried and begged for my mama to come back home. It hurt me so badly, and the days I got to see her were both the best and worst days of my life. Those were the days I'd count down to, the days I got to see one of my most favorite people. But it was also the day I'd have to say goodbye to her again. The days that they tried to pry me away from my mama while I screamed at the top of my lungs, begging to please let me stay with her. But it never worked out that way. Then, I'd have to go home and prepare to go to school the next day, where people loved making fun of me, and then I'd have to go to the after-school program, where my dad would stop by on his way to work to tell he loved me and he'd see me the next morning.

I cried and begged to go with him, too. Again, it never worked out that way. Then, my sister, who'd just moved to San Diego after graduating, came back home. My world lit up for a second. Then my mom came back home, and just as I thought it'd get better, it got a little worse. My mom and dad were having issues, so my mom decided to move out. At first, they said they were getting divorced, but they just separated for a little bit. When I was about nine or nine and a half, my parents settled things, and my mom moved back in. Now, they're so in love that if you saw them, you'd never believe what they went through!

~ A freshman student

CHAPTER

17

A Special Case

This is a letter one of my sophomore girls wrote to me. I noticed she was sad, and I asked her if she was okay. She didn't say anything, so I asked her to write me a letter and let me know what was going on.

I presented her case, anonymously, to some of my classes and received some beautiful letters of support for her that I have also included here. It turned out that she was wrong to believe that nobody cared.

NOBODY LIKES ME

Dear Mr. Landes,

I feel so alone and disappointed. I'm such a failure! I cut myself again. This time, I made more vertical cuts. I heard cutting vertically is better than horizontally, they can't stitch you up that way! I couldn't even go two weeks without doing some damage to myself. I couldn't help it! The first chance I get to be alone, I just do it. I'm addicted! I've been doing this for over a year now. I was doing well at keeping it a secret until people (my mom) started becoming suspicious. Each and every day, I get disappointed when I wake up! I wish I could fall asleep and never wake up. I don't cry anymore. I've gotten used to the pain. I've gotten used to slicing my skin. I don't even feel the sharpness of the razor anymore. Just relief. I'm sorry for not giving much detail to what's going on. I would rather not say. I just want somebody to listen to me and how I feel. I really hate myself sooo much. I don't see one thing about me to like. I'm an ugly, pathetic freak. I'm really scared my mom is going to see my fresh cuts. She always explodes and yells and tells me to "Just stop!" It's not that easy. She makes it seem like it's the easiest thing to do. But it's OK... I deserve the cuts. I deserve much more, though. It's still not enough. I need to cover every ugly fat inch of my body. I'm still debating whether or not to kill myself. This would be my fourth attempt. Maybe if I do it soon, I can avoid my mom, and she won't send me to an institution. Nobody would care. They would be happy to be rid of me. Maybe then people would hear me! They'd listen! I wish my thoughts would leave me alone! Please. I want the voices to go away. One question, though. Why? Today, some kid made fun of me picking my lip. I can't help my anxiety. Why is everyone so mean? Like this other kid who is so mean and rude to me. I don't know what I ever did to him. He just doesn't like me. LEAVE ME ALONE! Please! I feel bad enough already, you don't need to point out the things I am most insecure about. I hate having anxiety. Walking into the room just now, I almost started crying. There were so many eyes staring at me. They were probably wondering why I am so ugly and fat. You know one thing I hate? It just came to my head, but when people say they care about you, but when you need them, they're never there. I just have too many feelings right now. I'm tired of this, tired of feeling this way, tired of the same thing... tired of being tired.

P.S. I'm sorry for being behind on everything in class. It's just this other stuff has been getting to me and I can't focus. Thank you for listening and showing you care. It honestly means a lot!

~ A sophomore student

THE DODERMAN

Hello Mr. Landes,

I am the Doderman! For specific reasons, I will not allow you to know my real identity. I am in your class, but I'm not telling you which period I am in.

I am writing this letter in response to the suicidal girl mentioned this day.

My advice to her is this: I wish that she could one day open her eyes and see what is reality.

She is a very cute girl and not very overweight at all. If only she could just try to see what is reality and stop paying attention to the non-existent pictures she has drawn in her head.

On this, I so declare sincerely,
The Doderman
~ A freshman student

CUTTING BUTTERFLIES

Dear Mr. Landes,

I used to cut. I know how she feels. I did it for family reasons. The reason why I stopped was because I made a commitment to an amazing friend. He passed away. He committed suicide. We promised each other to never do it again, no matter how hard things would get. If we felt the need to cut, we would write it out, poetry, songs, or quotes. We would always talk to each other about our feelings. Now that he's gone, I don't really talk to people as much as I used to talk with him about my feelings. When he died, I wanted to cut, but I didn't. I tried a different method because the thought of cutting was getting stronger. I tried the butterfly method. All you have to do is draw a butterfly wherever you used to cut. It could be your arms, legs, or stomach. Wherever I cut. If you cut and have the butterfly, you kill that beautiful butterfly. Once it starts fading and you still feel like cutting, draw it again, and soon, you stop feeling the need of cutting.

For about six months, I had butterflies on my arms. It helped me a lot. It might just help her.

Sincerely,
~ A freshman student

ME, TOO

Dear Mr. Landes,

I used to cut. I smoke. I used to do drugs. I used to drink. I haven't cut in two months. I haven't smoked in two days. I haven't done any drugs in six months. I haven't drank in two months.

Why did I do all of that? Because when my mom was still alive, she hit me every day. So, I started cutting, smoking, drinking, and doing drugs. It made me feel better. I've attempted suicide.

I may seem happy on the outside, but on the inside, I feel like a total failure. I get picked on every day. I get called a whore, fat, hoe, ugly, and worthless. I know I'm none of these, but sometimes I sure feel like it!

I've been happy lately because I have an amazing, really sweet boyfriend.

I know how that girl in that letter feels. She just needs to ignore everyone who upsets her. She's worth it!

You inspire me to keep my head up and ignore bad things, and to try new things to change my life.

Thank you, Mr. Landes!

~ A freshman student

P.S. I'm going to quit smoking! :)

FREE HUGS

Dear Mr. Landes,

I almost forgot to tell you that I think your "Free Hugs" proposition on the door is something I've always respected you for. For the last two years, I've gone out to the mall with a few of my friends and stood there with signs and shirts. Ya, at first we felt stupid, but after a while, seeing people with a smile afterward, and even the people willing to help us, was a great feeling.

And as well, I'm guessing the girl and note you were talking about is my friend. If it is, thank you for helping her. She was really down today. And if it's not, thank you anyway, just for brightening the day of a potential friend!

Thank you.

~ A senior student

CHAPTER

18

Goals and Aspirations

The following letters helped me know the importance of being there for our kids. They have dreams, aspirations, and goals, and we need to be there to encourage them to reach for the stars!

Do you know what your child dreams of? Have you asked them? When they tell you their wild goals, how do you respond? Encourage them, no matter how unrealistic their aspirations may seem to you. Never scoff at their dreams or make fun of them. Who knows how far your child can go if they have the support of the people they need the most!

ACTOR

Dear Mr. Landes,

I'll be writing to you often. I have a goal! No one has ever told me I could reach my goals. Now that I have the mindset, NOTHING will stop me! HERE'S THE STORY!

I love James Patterson, best author ever! I was looking for his last Alex Cross novel when I went to a yard sale. I saw a book that said James Patterson. I assumed it was James's *Alex Cross*. I bought it. When I got home, it said *Maximum Ride, the Angel Experiment*. I was disappointed, but I read it and fell in love with it! I found out it was a series, so I read a lot of them. Then, just my luck, I found out they're making a movie of it!

So, I freak out. I went online to see how to make a resume. Then, I found out you need a professional headshot. My mom won't pay for it, and I can't get a job yet. So, I'm trying to get money for my birthday, which is September 29th. But I found out they haven't cast anyone for the movie yet.

I think this movie is my destiny. God brought me to that book. He's making them wait for me. No one has as much of a connection with that story as I do. I'll get my part in this story!

So, Mr. Landes, I'm asking you to help me stay true to my goal, to help me get there!

~ A sophomore student

GRADUATE

Dear Mr. Landes,

I'm glad I had you as a teacher this year. You've inspired me so much, and because of you, I'm gonna graduate and be successful!

~ Senior student

INSPIRATION

Dear Mr. Landes,

I'm so thankful to be in your class this year. I've learned so much, and you taught me how to be myself. I never believed in myself or that I could do anything. I always thought I was a failure. But thanks to you, I always push myself into doing things I thought I could never do. You truly are an inspiration. I'm sad that I won't have your class anymore, but I'll still come and visit you. Thanks for all of your help. You are one of my favorite teachers. God Bless You!

Love always,
~ Junior student

LIFE STORY

Dear Mr. Landes,

    I love my English class. You are a great motivational speaker, and you inspire me to read the affirmations and quotes! They make me feel so much better about myself. You have such good advice, and if I'm having a bad day, you tell us to do a good thing, and it will turn the day around! I always feel good coming to your classroom. I've learned a lot of good things already after only a week in your class. I am so glad I got switched into your class.

    You tell us to think about our future, and you tell us things to think about in regards to our future. I love writing. I write when I'm happy, excited, sad, mad, and when I need to vent. That's why I'm writing a book, and it's already about halfway done. It's only an eight-chapter book, and I'm almost done with the third chapter. Mr. Landes, you have told me a lot about life, and I'm going to use it in my book. My life story isn't even close to being done!

Thank you.
~ A freshman student

MY FUTURE

Dear Mr. Landes,

    I know I'm not the best student, but hearing you talk about life, and how you show us the inspirational videos, helps me a lot right now. Since I have many family problems going on right now. Thank you for letting me know that things will get better and to look forward to the future!! It means a lot!

Thank you,
~ A freshman student

CHAPTER

19

Taking Responsibility

One of the hardest parts of being a teacher is getting a person to do their work. I had a junior boy who had not passed a freshman or sophomore class, but he ended up graduating with his class. It took summer school, night school, and extended summer school, but he did it. He took responsibility for his actions.

It is essential that we model responsible behavior for our children and make them accountable for their choices. More often than not, they will surprise us with their maturity and desire to do what is right.

FORGIVE ME FOR LYING

Dear Mr. Landes,

On Monday, when you asked if we had our quotes that we write down off the board every day written down, I used my friend's quotes because I didn't have mine.

I'm sorry. If you want to take those points off my grade, I deserve it. I only did it because I know that my grade wasn't the best in the class. I am also writing this because I am ashamed of what I did, and I am truly sorry for lying to you.

If you want to talk to me, we can talk in person, face-to-face, but I am really embarrassed and ashamed of what I did. Forgive me. Like

I said, please remove those points from my grade because I didn't deserve them.

Thank you for taking your time in reading this.

I now don't have to feel guilty for lying!

Sincerely,
~ A sophomore student

MORE TIME

Dear Mr. Landes,

I was in the hospital with my little brother. They think his kidneys are bad, and I didn't get to finish my homework. Can I have a little time to do the homework and turn it in late?

~ A freshman student

PROCRASTINATION

Dear Mr. Landes,

I've obviously been having procrastination problems and I wanted to ask if I could do ANYTHING to raise my grade, but I'm honestly too embarrassed to ask in person. Please, if there is anything I can do, I will do it!

~ A junior boy

PS. Thank you for even taking the time to read this. I hope you have a great weekend.

I WORK TOO HARD

Dear Mr. Landes,

I didn't have time to do the Identity book project and the Family Heritage interviews because I work now. I haven't had a chance to do it since I work twelve hours every day. I left work early today so I can take some work to school today. This is my cell phone number so we can keep in touch.

Well, I have to go now. Thanks for everything. Text me

~ A junior student

CHAPTER

20

Fears

Our teens carry some real fears with them, from what will happen to pets to family concerns, and even fears of becoming homeless. These are not small matters, and as much as possible, we need to provide security and support to our kids to help them learn to deal with these kinds of major issues.

SICK HORSE

Dear Mr. Landes,

Hey there, Mr. Landes. I'm kinda sorta really stressed out. My black horse, Midnight, has been having a hard time breathing since last Friday. And yesterday, it got worse. The vet wants me to bring her in today. I'm paying for this vet bill with the money I have saved up for college. I have probably $1500 in there, and I talked to my grandma about this.

I told her that if my horse has strains of pneumonia, or if I have to spend over that amount of money, I'm going to have to put her to sleep.

I've had her for almost two years. She's my best friend. I don't want to lose her, but I also don't want her to suffer. But at the same time, I want to do everything I can to save her.

If I have to retire her, if I don't have to put her down, then I'll retire her. I'd do anything for that horse. I will text you if I take her to the vet tonight and let you know what's going to happen.

~ A freshman student

MOVING

Dear Mr. Landes,

I need your advice on how to react to my problem.

I may lose my house. We are renting it right now, and the owner is putting it up for sale. We don't have the money to buy the house, and we can't get a loan. So, we can't buy this house now or rent any other.

Dad doesn't have any idea what we're going to do if we lose our house. I'm worried that he might want to move out of state, or down to Southern California, all because of his girlfriend.

I don't know if I should start packing up my room or what? I'm just really confused as to what to do.

~ A sophomore student

MONEY PROBLEMS

Dear Mr. Landes,

My situation is getting worse and worse. Our house is for rent, and our landlords are going to sell our house. My dad has been unemployed for more than ten months now, and we could have a little more than a month to move. We may have to move in with our grandparents, and I don't want to move. I'm not going to let this get me in a bad mood. That's why I'm writing this. I hope that things will turn out alright. But I know God's plans have obstacles. On top of all of this, my parents are still supporting my soccer. I feel bad that this takes up money. It hurts me to see my mom worried. She's a strong woman, and she won't show us what she is really thinking, and my dad feels awful for not being able to support me and my family. I think that we are going to look over the web and paper and search for houses over winter break. Mr. Landes, I don't want you to feel bad for me. I just needed to write to get it out. Thanks so much for listening.

P.S. My mom feels bad with the holidays coming up and our landowners are going to try to sell our house. So, while we are still living in it, we have to let people come to check it out. Plus, we have three dogs, and we have to get rid of them to move.

~ A freshman student

WHERE WILL WE LIVE

Dear Mr. Landes,

If I seem upset, it is because yesterday morning, I found out that my stepdad has been cheating on my mom. Then, I got a phone call from my sister, saying my real dad is in jail for physically abusing my stepmom.

Not only was all of that hard to hear, but both of them were the only income of money to my mom, so we will probably end up losing our house, and I don't know where we will be living.

~ A junior student

WORRIED ABOUT FAMILY

Dear Mr. Landes,

I'm sad because my eighty-two-year-old grandma is not doing so well. She had a stroke and it paralyzed her whole left side of her body, and it's hard seeing her so miserable. She can't walk anywhere with us anymore.

I hate it so much, and then my mom is not feeling so good. I'm constantly driving her to the hospital because she gets chest pains and has trouble breathing. It sucks a lot having to see them go through so much pain. Hopefully, they will get better soon, and when they are better, I'll be OK!

Thanks for caring,
~ A freshman student

WORRIED ABOUT MY FRIEND

Dear Mr. Landes,

I'm really worried about my friend. She was texting me two days ago, and she had been telling me she had tried committing suicide, and I guess her mom took her to a psychiatric hospital, and I'm guessing she is staying there.

She's been out this entire week so far. I've tried texting her, and I get no response. I called her, and her phone went straight to her voicemail.

I'm praying to God that she's OK. It's almost like she's slowly starting to follow in my footsteps. Please keep her in your prayers. She's like a little sister to me, and I love her to death.

Thank you for everything,
~ A junior student

VOICES

PLEASE DON'T TELL!!

Dear Mr. Landes,

I don't know how to tell you this. I'm really scared to tell you. You can't tell. I'm in a lot of trouble if my mom finds out. Well, here goes…

On Sunday night, I was sitting in my room. All of a sudden, I got flashbacks. My past went through my head, then I got a voice in my head. It told me to grab this shoelace and wrap it around my neck and pull. (Before all of this happened, I texted my friend) The voice told me not to let go until my friend texted back. A few seconds later, I got her text, but the voice told me to keep pulling, but then, I let go.

It happened fast. If my mom finds out… I don't want to even think of her finding out. But I'm fine now. I don't have the strength to go all the way.

PLEASE DON'T TELL!!

~ A freshman student

CHAPTER

21

Pain

Sometimes the letters students write to me are shocking. The pain some of these kids carry is devastating, and often the result of a less-than-wonderful home environment and a serious lack of parental support. Cutting is a common way for these kids—especially girls—to alleviate that pain. Students who are cutting, suicidal, or dealing with abuse and neglect need specialized care and so much love. Here are some of their stories:

CUTTING

Dear Mr. Landes,

What is up with me today is that things were going on yesterday, and I was crying and just having a bad day, and what I did to release my stress and anger was that I cut my left wrist four times, but only one or so showed up. Even though I have friends who help me with my problems, the ones that go here are... My other friends who help me are Phillip, Monica, and Tony. And they go to Salida Middle School. The last person is my cousin. At least I have you as a teacher, who tries to help me with things.

~ A freshman student

STRESSED OUT

Dear Mr. Landes,

Today I am having a very stressful day, and I am on the verge of crying at this point.

I am ready to cut myself again, but I know it's not the best thing. But to me, it feels like I have to. I am just very depressed today. I really need someone to cheer me up, and you're the best person to cheer people up. I really need help at this point. I really just want to lose my mind. I just want to hide from life and never come out.

All of my stress started today during 4th period. It is stressing me out so much. I just don't know how much more stress I can take anymore. My life feels like a tornado at times. I just feel so broken right now!

Your student,
~ A freshman student

LOCKED UP

Dear Mr. Landes,

Thank you for writing me and sending those words of encouragement. Also, thank you for letting my cousin write me. That made me feel good and surprised me.

I got the letter nine days after you sent it, and I'm writing you the day after Thanksgiving. They served ham and stuffing, which was surprising, but I didn't eat. I rarely eat dinner, and I'm starting to not eat breakfast. I've lost a lot of weight. I've been down (locked up) for five months, so I'm tired of the food.

I'm in a welding class, and I'm pretty good at it. I'm going on my fourth week, and I've passed a test. When I'm sober, I get so much accomplished. I've made a commitment to serve God in a covenant with him. Some of the inmates call me Rev. because I'm in a prayer circle within my barracks that prays for everyone and reads certain verses out of the Bible, which the Spirit leads me to pick. Make sure my little cousin is alright, Landes. Thank you very much. Write back soon.

Much Love,
~ A former student

P.S. If you can send money, that would help.

I CAN'T FORGET ABOUT MY PAST

Dear Mr. Landes,

I think you can help me.

I'm trying to forget about my past, but I can't. It makes me miserable, and I don't know what to do.

Sometimes, I feel lonely and insecure, and I'm not happy, but I don't know what's making me unhappy.

Please keep this private. If you have some advice, please write back.

Do you think God will forgive me for what we've done in our past?

~ A junior student

RAPE

Dear Mr. Landes,

When you mentioned that you had a student who was the product of a rape, that surprised me. My birth mom was raped when she was sixteen, and she had me at seventeen and put me up for adoption. The mom who adopted me is the only mom I have ever known. She tells me every single day she is glad God chose her to be my mom. I'll never know if my birth mom was telling the truth about her rape. I read it on my adoption files. My birth dad wrote on the paper that he didn't want to meet me. I met my birth mom when I was eight, and right before my ninth birthday, she and her son came to visit me. The parents who adopted me had already divorced, and my birth mom came to my dad's house. The dad who adopted me slept with my birth mom. The next morning, my birth mom was gone. And I haven't talked to her since then. She blackmails her parents and family to not talk to me. This is the reason I don't like my dad. The only reason I deal with my dad is because I don't want my brother to have to deal with my dad by himself. My brother was also adopted, but our birth family talks to him almost every day. I hope this helps you to understand me more.

    I try to not let it get me down because my mom is my whole world. But there isn't a day that goes by where I don't think about my birth mom. I have gone to church to try to forgive my dad, but I am not strong enough to forgive him. He lies to me and tells me all the time how little I am worth and how I will become nothing. I don't hate him. I love him only because he is my dad, but there are times I wish he wasn't. But when I think that, I feel guilty. Don't feel different towards me. I just felt like letting you know.

~ A junior student

USED AND ABUSED

Dear Mr. Landes,

    Lately, I'm starting to feel like I have no hope toward relationships. I used to feel confident about them, but that confidence is long gone. I'm starting to feel insecure about my appearance, and also my body. I lost five pounds, shockingly. I very much long to weigh more! But... the opposite happened. I really want to weigh 115, but I'm now 105. I hate myself. I started doing butt workouts the summer before my sophomore year last year, and I had the perfect behind! It was toned, lifted, bubbly, just perfect! For some reason, it's shrinking. In freshman year, these two popular girls made up a rumor about me that I wore butt pads, and soon the rumor spread throughout the entire school. I lost friends because they were embarrassed to be seen with me. For a while, I would eat lunch in the J building bathroom stalls. I had no one. I was a slutty joke to everyone. I finally posted a picture of myself on Facebook, explaining this rumor. I got almost 200 likes on it. The rumor finally died down. Thank God.

    Back to my other issue; I tend to look for boys who will use me for sex, then never talk to me again. I can't even remember an estimate of all the guys that I've gone through obsessing over sex from me. To myself, I feel that I pick the wrong, disrespectful, abusive, bitter, hypocritical boys because that's how my dad is to me. So, I've grown into a teenager thinking that "if I want a boy, they need to be just like my dad." But my dad has also encouraged me to find a guy like him... I have no hope. I've been single for far too long, used and abused way too much.

~ A sophomore student

BURNS

Dear Mr. Landes,

You ask for one more day, one more hour, one more minute. That is one more day of suffering. I am not like other girls. I don't hate myself because I am fat, or that other people judge me because of that, or that other people judge me.

Most of that. I am over. I am me and no one different. I do/did have my other reasons.

I have attempted suicide, and once, I did major damage and my ex walked in and saved me. At this point in my life, I don't want to kill myself. But I am hurting and suffering, and I don't know how to ask for help sometimes.

I admit that I need help. I walk around like I'm fine, like my only problem is "I broke a reed in band" or "I didn't have time to flat iron my hair!" When, honestly, I am dying on the inside. All the burns on my arms and the scars on my legs remind me of what I've gone through, which doesn't help, even if I weighed 100 pounds. I would never be able to wear a swimsuit because of all the damage I used to do to myself.

I feel as though this class is so uplifting, from the videos to just how you share your life experiences. And I thought I would share some of my own, and thank you!

~ A sophomore student

PUNISHMENT

Dear Mr. Landes,

    I was wondering, if my parents threaten to hit me with a belt, poke me in the eye, hit me with a wooden spoon, take my phone away, and only have nothing to do when bored. Is it good parenting to be threatening me with these things? I am wondering because my parents threaten me like this.

    ~ Freshman student

CHAPTER

22

Heroes

Still not sure why we need to be champions for our kids? These next letters will help you understand! We NEED to be champions for our kids!

ALL BY MYSELF

Dear Mr. Landes,

The person I once admired was my oldest sister because of her successes in life. She was the first in my family to get a real job besides prostitution or drug dealing. She was the first to finish and graduate from high school. She went to Kitchen Academy and received her diploma as a nursing assistant.

My oldest sister taught me and showed me that I determine my decisions and goals in life. No matter the predicaments I struggle with, I can become what I want. My sister finished it all by age twenty-one. But now she hardly talks to me or sees me because she's dating my mother's ex-boyfriend, who is the stepdad of my ex.

I've learned to rely on and inspire myself because only I can lead and control my own success. My sister taught me not to depend on anyone or trust, because at the end, it'll only be me, myself, and I. Things have been hard being alone since age twelve. I've been in twenty-seven foster homes, three group homes, one twice, a mental hospital, once for suicide, and the receiving home seven times within the last five years.

I'm still looking for love or someone to inspire me, but it's hard because I don't trust anybody, even family. I've been put down by so many people. I don't even really know when to let go, but I do know I can do better all by myself, and I don't need anybody trying to hold me down.

~ A junior student

MY HERO

Dear Mr. Landes,

1. He always gives hugs to people for fun.
2. He is always here to talk to us when we are down.
3. He gives great advice when we're going through trouble.

My hero is a teacher, and his name is Mr. Landes. He is my hero because he gives hugs, talks to us when we are down, and he gives us great advice when we are in trouble.

Every day, when people come to school, Mr. Landes will be waiting outside his door to give hugs to people. He changes people's lives with his hugs, because most people don't receive hugs from home. No matter if you're a girl or a boy, he will give hugs. If you're sad or upset and just need a hug, Mr. Landes is there, and he will give you a hug!

When people go home, they go through trouble with their parents or family members. A student comes to school, and Mr. Landes is all here for you. He always listens to you when you are hurting. When he is teaching a class, and you come to his class, he stops his class to listen to you. No matter what he is doing, he will stop to listen because he loves you.

When people get in trouble at home and they don't know what to do, they come to Mr. Landes, and he always knows what to tell them. He wants to see us live a great life. He loves to help people and give advice because he has seen kids' lives get ruined, and he doesn't want to see our lives look like theirs!

Now, since you have read this, you know why Mr. Landes is my hero. He is my hero because he gives hugs, talks to us when we are down, and gives great advice.

~ A junior student

KEEPING HOPE

Dear Mr. Landes,

Thank you so much for coming last night, Mr. Landes. I know I didn't talk much to you, but just your being there for me meant a lot! As you can tell, I'm having a lot of problems at home and at school. But all the things you tell us really go deep in my heart. The way you think and talk to us really did change me.

I really do think you are the best teacher in the world, and I know God will give you a lot of things in return. I am so lucky to have someone like you in my life. I just wish I would have met you a long time ago. I know I haven't known you for a long time, but just for a couple of days, but I know you are the type of person who cares about people. I would really like to be like you in the future! The way you see life is so positive. Every time I try, someone always has to come along and push me down, and when I get back up, someone else does it again. But you know what? I'm not going to give up because, like you say, this is part of the game. Sometimes, I really do wish it could end.

Last night, I spent a lot of time thinking about your words and decided to change and always give my best! I would wake up with a smile and go to bed with a smile on my face!

But for what had to happen today, my hopes came down just like my smile. I just want to reach my dreams and goals and make myself and my family happy because I love them. If you could help me in this, I would be really grateful.

Thank you for everything, Mr. Landes. I can't give you much in return but my friendship and trust, but trust me, you'll always get a smile, no matter how down I am. Thank you once again!

~ A junior student

PS. This isn't a perfect English letter, but it is from the heart, and I will make it up to you with my work!

LIFE TEACHER

Dear Mr. Landes,

    For my free write, I just wanted to say, I have had an awesome year with you as my teacher. You have taught me things this year that I haven't learned before, like: Trying to stay positive no matter what happens, not to settle for less, and that people will judge you on your appearance.

    This year, I have made new friends, and some I've even gotten closer with. That wouldn't be possible without your teachings. I'm going to miss you when I go on and be a Junior next year. But I promise that I'll come and visit your classroom once in a while and check up to see how things are going.

    Thank you for being my teacher in life and in English.

~ A sophomore boy (resource student)

P.S. I am very proud of you because I can see how you change people's lives every day, including mine. Every time I come into your classroom, you've always managed to make me smile, and I really like that, and you also make me feel good about myself. By the way, I have to say you have an amazing voice. I love it when you sing in class. Every time you sing, I want to sing, too! Thank you for everything.

CHANGED!

Mr. Landes,

You truly are the best inspiration I ever could've had. I was a wreck in this world and full of hatred and regret of unaccomplished things that I wanted to be part of. I was going down a bad path of aggressive behavior and really hard times, but I've noticed that after your class and all your many speeches on human kindness and our power to overcome the largest mountains, my life has become a lot more clear, and I'm now a passive but firm person that fights for the needy and laughs at the greedy. I help the fallen and recruit the flying to do as I do. I give the people that feel as if they're at their lowest a path to the stairs of success and show them the railing from which they may lay to rest themselves on the way up. And because of you, my life has been blessed and full of adventure. So, Thank you, Mr. Landes. You're the best.

~ A freshman student

SAFE HAVEN

What I've gained from Mr. Landes.

From Mr. Landes, I've learned many things. He's also changed my life. He has helped me become a better person, the person I've been looking for.

He taught me that there will be hurt, but you can't hold on to that. He's reassured me that all I've been through, I will survive. Coming to Mr. Landes's class, I am home. I love it here more than my own house. I am comfortable here, not being called fat, ugly, lazy, and worthless.

In Mr. Landes's class, I am someone who counts and is a part of the class. But once I walk out of here, I'm nothing. Although Mr. Landes teaches me all of this, I still leave knowing I am a person my mother or anyone else will never like.

~ A freshman student

THANK YOU

Hi Mr. Landes,

    I just wanted to thank you for all that you've done and for helping me through. Things have been much better at home, and I now have a boyfriend! His name is… He is in your 1st period. :) You're an amazing teacher, and you've taught me so much!

~ A sophomore student

WHO HAS MADE A DIFFERENCE IN YOUR LIFE

I believe that you make a difference in all of our lives. I have noticed that there is a positive energy in this classroom that is not present in most. The lessons you teach make me think more deeply on how I live my life and understand the true meaning of making a difference.

    It is amazing what one person can do for another, and I can bet that hundreds of lives will be changed for the better due to the lessons that you have given to us. The way you teach is impressive because it permanently engraves a positive outlook into the listener's head and enables them to think for themselves on how to be a better person. Thanks for making a difference!

~ A senior student

GIFT OF WORDS

Dear Mr. Landes,

    I appreciate how you open up with your outlook on everything, and do not act in a narrow-minded manner.

    I mean, some would have one or three self-help and success books, but you try to get all the good books you can, and it has helped me realize that no matter my past, I do deserve the best and shouldn't settle for being "OK" or "just good."

So, just know that while half the first-period class is still tired, I AM listening and using what you give as a gift with your words!

Thank you!
~ A senior student

BEING YOUR OWN HERO

Dear Mr. Landes,

So, unfortunately, the meeting with my mom, my sister, you, and myself isn't going to happen.

Things keep getting worse. Not with me, just family things in general. Now, my mom is taking my oldest sister to court to take her children away from her. Which, to me, I think is dumb because she has no reason to.

But I used to be so determined to do good in my life and to graduate for my family, because they always used to tell me I couldn't do it, that I was going to be like my oldest sister and drop out, have kids at a young age, and not have a decent job.

But now, I realize I am doing it for me. From now on, I am going to prove them all wrong. I am no longer going to be weak, as much as it's a lot for a teenager like me to deal with. I know I can get through it, thanks to you.

But I have decided to stay away from all that family drama, as much as I love my mom. Of course, I will always love her, no matter what we go through. Just right now, I'm going to let things calm down.

But I wanted to thank you for everything. Always being there when I need someone to talk to about a problem... and I know I probably will have more problems than a math book. Also, I wanted to thank you for making me stronger. You honestly have, and you've taught me a lot about life, especially to be strong.

So, thank you for everything. I am so lucky to have met you and to have you as a part of my life.

~ A senior student

CHAPTER 23

Prayers

Students are often curious about faith. Some are raised with it, but for far too many, it is a foreign concept, but one they are eager to learn about. Faith and prayer can offer children security, guidance, and comfort, regardless of the religion being taught.

I remember teaching at a school, and a boy asked me, "How do you know what is the right religion, right church, right anything?" I told him then, as I still believe now, "A true seeker will always find truth!" I've taught students of many different religions, faiths, and beliefs, and I have loved them all!

SHAKEN FAITH

Dear Mr. Landes,

Thank you for your encouragement. I really need the push right now. Your faith is strong, but I'm losing mine. I know it's a test and I need to stay strong, and it's so easy to just break down and just give up, but I don't want to. Please keep me in your prayers, as you are in mine!

Sincerely,
~ A senior student

DEAR MR. LANDES

ANONYMOUS PRAYER

Dear Mr. Landes,

I promise that I will keep you and your mom in my prayers. I feel that God is going to bless your mother. She will rise over this cancer. Tell your mother not to give up. Tell her that she will be in my prayers. And tell your mother to be strong and keep asking God to help, and he will open the door.

I love you guys! Don't give up!

Stay strong!

Love always,
~ Signed Unknown

PS. When I need a little kick when I'm down, I listen to *Imagine Me* by Kurt Franklin.

COULD YOU PRAY

Dear Mr. Landes,

I know that you are a religious man, and I'm asking that you pray for my mother, who was admitted to the hospital today with a skin infection.

Thank you,
~ A freshman student

HOUSE ARREST

Dear Mr. Landes,

I need prayer, big time. I'm going through a lot right now. I did stuff, not good, and now it feels like my parents don't want me. It feels like I'm on house arrest. I'm a foster kid, and I've never had a dad before.

Now I have a stepdad, and I don't really pay attention to him because he's not my dad. My parents said to me that they don't know who I am anymore. They are so strict. They said I have to break up with my boyfriend, and we have been dating for six and a half months. I'm not going to. They know how much I like him. He means a lot to me.

They always have something bad for me. I feel alone every day. My boyfriend makes me feel like I'm someone. He always tells me how pretty I am or how beautiful I am. I never like to be at home. I don't know what to do anymore. I don't want my parents to know that I am telling you anything. Please don't tell.

~ A junior student

PRAYERS REQUESTED

Dear Mr. Landes,

I was wondering if you could keep my friend in prayer. Her name is… Her dad beat the crap out of her over the weekend. She is staying with her cousin this week. I told her if she wanted to, she could stay with me. I told her she isn't alone. Me and God are with her.

But I need you to pray for her. She has a black eye and everything. But she is in my prayers, and I was wondering if she could be in yours.

Sincerely,
~ A junior student

PRAYERS ON THE BUS

Dear Mr. Landes,

On the bus
I think a lot, and I'm thankful for my brain. I think about my day ahead, I think of my past, I fill my head with calm music, Trance or Christian. I read the Bible on my iPhone. I sit alone, I share my seat. Either way, I have a place to sit, and I see a lot. I'm thankful for my eyes.

DEAR MR. LANDES

As I look out the window, I see a man sweeping his porch, keeping his old, beautiful white house in good shape. I see a mother coughing at the stoplight. I say a prayer for her. I see a man at the side of a building, painting over graffiti. I see determined marathon joggers, I see the homeless sleeping in the park, I see a cemetery filled with enormous gravestones, and tiny ones, too. I see early morning coffee shop workers trying to make a living. I realize I am blessed. I arrive.

Your observant student,
~ A senior student

A CHECKLIST FOR DEALING WITH TEENS

Are you ready to do some self-evaluation? If not, why not? Read through the list and try to check off at least five of these each day. If you can't, try harder. Your kids are depending on you to step up your game. They need you to be present, approachable, safe, and consistent.

And remember, we all have tough days with our teens. If everything falls apart, don't beat yourself up. Pick up the pieces and try again. Apologize, communicate your honest feelings without blaming, and try again. These are hard years to get through, but your efforts will be rewarded with a healthy, happy adult who is able to cope with the world, has strong relationships, and includes you in their adult lives willingly and lovingly.

- ☐ Have I asked them about their day? Am I involved in my teenager's life? Too much or not enough?
- ☐ Do I really listen and pay attention to what they are saying, or not saying? Can I listen without preconceived opinions? Can I listen carefully without responding?
- ☐ Do I show true love and respect?
- ☐ Do they know they are loved? Have I asked them?
- ☐ How do I react and respond to testing? Before I say or do anything, do I ask myself, "Who is the adult?"
- ☐ Am I teaching them life lessons?
- ☐ Do I help them reach their highest goals?
- ☐ Do I know what their goals are?
- ☐ Am I proud of them? Do I tell them? Do they know?

- ☐ Do I seek the lesson amidst the mistake?
- ☐ Do I forgive and forget?
- ☐ Do I help them pick up the pieces, or do I make it worse?
- ☐ Do I remember my teenage years?
- ☐ Do I encourage bad behavior? Is their behavior a desperate attempt at attention?
- ☐ Do I push or encourage my teen? Do I see them as more than they are currently? Do I help them dream big?
- ☐ Am I a competent adviser?
- ☐ Am I behind them all the way? Do they know it?
- ☐ When was the last time I hugged my teen?
- ☐ Do they experience positive physical contact?
- ☐ Do I require my teen to be responsible? What chores could they do?
- ☐ Do I expect excellence? Do I help them achieve it?
- ☐ Do I show mercy and grace?
- ☐ Do I encourage them with my words and actions, or belittle and discourage them?
- ☐ Do I laugh with them rather than at them?
- ☐ Do we have fun together? Do I know what they consider fun?
- ☐ Am I willing to be with them?
- ☐ Do I ask them what they would like to do?
- ☐ Do I treat them as valuable, or as a nuisance?
- ☐ Do I talk with them, or at them?
- ☐ Do I treat them as young adults, capable of greatness?
- ☐ Am I willing to teach and learn, as well?
- ☐ Do I compliment my teens sincerely?
- ☐ Do I challenge my teen to be great without deflating or discouraging them?
- ☐ What is my definition of greatness? Does it matter if my definition is different than my teens?
- ☐ How will I respond if they never meet my standard?
- ☐ Do I love them unconditionally, even if?
- ☐ Do I bribe them or manipulate them?
- ☐ If they disappoint me or embarrass me, do I withhold my love? Do I expect something I never give?

- ☐ Do I expect my teen to take responsibility for their behavior?
- ☐ Have I asked my teen what I can do to be a better parent?
- ☐ Do I encourage my teen to read? Do I model good reading habits? Do I share what I have read with them recently? Have I shared with them my favorite books or poems lately, or ever?
- ☐ Do I notice little things about my teen? Are they nervous, scared, withdrawn, lonely, bored? If they are, what am I willing to do to help them?
- ☐ Do they have real friends? Do they know what a real friend is? Am I that real friend they can always rely on?
- ☐ Do I pray for my teen? Do I let them know I'm praying for them? They NEED to know! Ask them to pray for you.
- ☐ When was the last time I showed my teen my love? When did I last tell them? I need to tell them and show them again and again and again... and then again and again!
- ☐ What is my truth? Can I share it with my teen? If not, why not?
- ☐ Do I notice things that are well done, or do I only criticize their mistakes?
- ☐ Do I tease them playfully and lovingly? NEVER be sarcastic, or hit their hot buttons or vulnerabilities!
- ☐ Do I encourage them about their futures?
- ☐ Do they know they can count on me in their hardest moments? Why or why not?
- ☐ Do I teach them things they need to know to be successful? Do I give them opportunities and resources to become successful?
- ☐ Am I a good role model in my behavior, language, and actions? Do I expect what I fail to deliver?
- ☐ I am aware that I am being watched by my teen.

I BELIEVE

People are the most valuable resource on the planet.

Every student has tremendous potential, is teachable, and can learn.

Everyone can succeed in reaching their goals and living out their dreams.

Any school I teach at is the best school in the world.

Communication is the most underrated skill in today's society.

I have the best students in the school.

A smile is a universal language that transcends from the heart.

I can make a difference in your life, and you will make a difference in mine!

ABOUT THE AUTHOR

Photo by Lexi Sleeman

Rod Landes taught for twenty-seven years in the Modesto Public School system. He taught at every public school in the district, some for only summer school and short stints, and at others, such as Gregori and Johansen, for several years. He has also worked as a motivational speaker and enjoys lifting and encouraging others.

At six feet, six inches tall, Rod knows what it's like to be singled out. He hated school, was an unmotivated student, and suffered from low self-esteem. As a teacher, he strongly related to his students and could easily identify with the messages in the letters they wrote to him. He credits this empathy and relatability to his success as a 'favorite teacher' of many students.

Rod has two sons and two stepchildren. He is happily married to Debbie.

www.ingramcontent.com/pod-product-compliance
Lightning Source LLC
Chambersburg PA
CBHW030221170426
43194CB00007BA/818